Your Secret Charisma

How to Repair Business and Personal Relationships – and Gain Trust and Forgiveness for Success, Happiness and Fulfillment

Tom Marcoux

America's Communication Coach
TFG Thought Leader
Speaker-Author of 23 books
Blogger, BeHeardandBeTrusted.com

A QuickBreakthrough Publishing Edition

Copyright © 2014 Tom Marcoux Media, LLC
ISBN: 0692210962
ISBN-13: 978-0692210963

All rights reserved. No part of this book may be reproduced or transmitted in any form by any means electronic or mechanical, including photocopying, recording or by any information storage and retrieval system without written permission from the publisher.

QuickBreakthrough Publishing is an imprint of Tom Marcoux Media, LLC. More copies are available from the publisher, Tom Marcoux Media, LLC. Please call (415) 572-6609 or write TomSuperCoach@gmail.com

or visit www.TomSuperCoach.com

or Tom's blog: www.BeHeardandBeTrusted.com

This book was developed and written with care. Names and details were modified to respect privacy.

Disclaimer: The author and publisher acknowledge that each person's situation is unique, and that readers have full responsibility to seek consultations with health, financial, spiritual and legal professionals. The author and publisher make no representations or warranties of any kind, and the author and publisher shall not be liable for any special, consequential or exemplary damages resulting, in whole or in part, from the reader's use of, or reliance upon, this material.:

Other Books by Tom Marcoux:
- Be Heard and Be Trusted: How to Get What You Want
- Nothing Can Stop You This Year!
- Darkest Secrets of Persuasion and Seduction Masters
- Darkest Secrets of Charisma
- Darkest Secrets of Negotiation Masters
- Darkest Secrets of the Film and Television Industry Every Actor Should Know
- Darkest Secrets of Making a Pitch to the Film and Television Industry
- Darkest Secrets of Film Directing
- Truth No One Will Tell You

Praise for *Your Secret Charisma*
• "Tom Marcoux reveals secrets so you can get anyone to forgive you and create warm feelings." – Dr. JoAnn Dahlkoetter, author of *Your Performing Edge* and coach to CEOs and Olympic Gold Medalists
• "Tom Marcoux is a master at understanding and managing relationships, and this book takes a fresh new approach. By focusing on how to repair damaged or broken relationships, Marcoux keys in on a critical but delicate topic that is relevant in both personal and business contexts...There's actionable value for everyone." – Paul Gillin, co-author of *Social Marketing to the Business Customer: Listen to Your B2B Market, Generate Major Account Leads, and Build Client Relationships*
• "*Your Secret Charisma* gives you the vital piece of charisma that is often missing. That piece is what Tom Marcoux calls Warm Trust Charisma. He goes beyond teaching you how to be attractive to guiding you to create warm and real business and personal relationships."
– Danek S. Kaus, author of *You Can Be Famous: Insider Secrets...*
• "You'll be inspired by Tom Marcoux's sincere efforts to help you resolve problems. I recommend this book to anyone in a pickle."
– David Barron, co-author of *Power Persuasion*

Praise for Tom Marcoux's Other Work:
• "In *Reduce Clutter, Enlarge Your Life*, Marcoux will help you get rid of the physical and mental clutter occupying precious space in your life. You'll reclaim wasted energy, lower your stress, and find time for new opportunities." – Laura Stack, author of *Execution IS the Strategy*
• "*Create Your Best Life* helps you learn skills in persuasion, charisma, confidence, influence and emotional strength. To make a dream come true, you'll need to get people enrolled in your vision. This is *the book* that helps you get great things done!" – Dr. JoAnn Dahlkoetter, author of *Your Performing Edge* and coach to CEOs and Olympic Gold Medalists
• "In *Darkest Secrets of Persuasion and Seduction Masters*, learn useful countermeasures to protect you from being darkly manipulated."
– David Barron, co-author, *Power Persuasion*
• "In *Be Heard and Be Trusted*, Tom's advice on how to remain true to yourself and establish authentic rapport with clients is both insightful and reality based. He [shows how] to establish oneself as a credible expert."
-Arthur P. Ciaramicoli, Ed.D., Ph.D., author *The Curse of the Capable*
• "*Nothing Can Stop You This Year* is a treasure trove of tips, tools, and terrific ideas—practical, reassuring, and energizing! Tom provides wonderful resources for achieving your goals." – Elayne Savage, Ph.D., author of *Don't Take It Personally! The Art of Dealing with Rejection*

Visit Tom's blog: www.BeHeardandBeTrusted.com

Tom Marcoux

CONTENTS

Dedication and Acknowledgments	I
Chapter One: Unleash Your Charisma through the I.N.F.L.U.E.N.C.E Process	7
Chapter Two: Influence through Energy, Poise, and Charisma (How to Heal When Life's Too Much)	59
Chapter Three: Say "Yes" to Yourself (Reduce Stress and Increase Ease)	91
Chapter Four: Work Effectively with Creditors (Get out of Debt and Back on Your Feet)	121
Chapter Five: Give It a Rest	143
Bonus Section #1 Your "Power of Five"	155
Bonus Section #2: Strengthen Yourself	173
A Final Word and Springboard to Your Success	189
Excerpt from *Darkest Secrets of Persuasion and Seduction Masters: How to Protect Yourself and Turn the Power to Good*	192
About the Author Tom Marcoux	200
Special Offer Just for Readers of this Book	202

DEDICATION AND ACKNOWLEDGEMENTS

This book is dedicated to the terrific book and film consultant, and author Johanna E. Mac Leod. It is also dedicated to the other team members. Thanks to Linda L. Chappo, Jill Ronsley (SunEditWrite.com) and Sherry Lusk for editing. Thanks to Johanna E. Mac Leod for rendering this book's front and back covers. Thanks to my father, Al Marcoux, for his concern and efforts for me. Thanks to my mother, Sumiyo Marcoux, a kind, generous soul. Thank you to Higher Power. Thanks to our readers, audiences, clients, my graduate/college students and my team members of Tom Marcoux Media, LLC. The best to you.

CHAPTER ONE: UNLEASH YOUR CHARISMA THROUGH THE I.N.F.L.U.E.N.C.E PROCESS

If you were charismatic, what could you accomplish? What cooperation would you get? How would your life get better if people genuinely trusted and liked you?

When many of us talk about charisma, we're only talking about what I call *Magnetic Charisma*. That's the compelling kind in which a charismatic person pulls you in.

This book is about *another* form of charisma: What I call *Warm Trust Charisma*. This is the form of charisma that gives you the true and long-term relationships that create personal fulfillment and success. If you're going to go far in business, you need people to trust you.

Since everyone makes mistakes you need Warm Trust Charisma to ride out the bumpy times in business and personal relationships. That's when you can lose that precious trust. **Can you repair any business or personal relationship?** With this book you'll learn how. I also refer to Warm Trust Charisma as **Your Secret Charisma**, because it's a form of charisma that is quiet. On the other hand, Magnetic Charisma can feel intimidating. You may feel attracted to some movie star but do you trust that person to pay your mortgage or help you get a good job?

Warm Trust Charisma consists of doing what makes people feel both comfortable and cooperative in your presence. The problem with Magnetic Charisma is that its power may fade with the length of time people are together. But Warm Trust Charisma deepens, if you know how to strengthen a relationship.

Here's a brief summary of the distinction between the two forms of Charisma:

Magnetic Charisma **attracts**.

Warm Trust Charisma **gains cooperation** for the long term.

This book is in your hands because I got in trouble—big, serious trouble. My elderly father was angry with me and he had cut off communication. It was then I realized that my father, who was 71 years old, had limited time left on this planet. I could not wait for him to change.

I had seen someone die in front of me and had known several people who died, so I felt an urgency to keep my relationships in a healthy and positive condition. The healing of the relationship with my father was in my hands.

The technique I used to resolve the situation with my father I will reveal later (in "Flex Your Options"), but it was one of the new and different methods to restore relationships that you will learn from this book.

Other books on charisma, persuasion and influence often focus on the context of sales and, even, politics. Here we focus on the times when influence is absolutely crucial to *restore* a relationship, friendship or conversation with a prospective customer. You may even need to restore your relationship with your boss or you may be fired.

This book will help you when you:
- Need to be forgiven
- Made a blunder with a prospective customer
- Need to make up for a mistake with a current customer
- Have lost the trust of a dear friend
- Realize your relationship is faltering and you did not even do anything wrong
- Need to work effectively with creditors so you can get out of debt and back on your feet

This material will even help a spouse to repair and restore a marriage.

An interviewer once asked me about this claim, saying, "That's a big thing to look at."

I replied, "We're talking about restoring trust. We're also looking at how to listen to another person so that he or she can express all the pain and know deep down that you care."

We will use the I.N.F.L.U.E.N.C.E. process:

I – Inquire
N – Nurture
F – Flex your options
L – Listen
U – Understand
E – Energize
N – Negotiate
C – Create (not compete)
E – Embrace

I will refer to the person you want to influence as the offended person. The whole idea is you made a mistake or blunder that has caused damage in the relationship. And now, the offended person associates even talking to you with pain. You want to restore the relationship and help the person trust you again.

In this section, you will learn how to practice the Secret Influence Process, which includes how to:
- Strengthen yourself
- Remain in a calm state of being
- Communicate your concern and kindness
- Take action with the F.A.R. (forgiveness, amends, regret) methods

In the upcoming sections, you'll learn to apply all four elements, and then you'll be able to radiate Your Secret Charisma (your Warm Trust Charisma). Remember that you need advanced relationship skills so that you create and protect relationships that are your source of opportunities that bring financial abundance and fulfillment. Let's begin…

INQUIRE
(#1 of the I.N.F.L.U.E.N.C.E. Process)

How can you take action towards restoring a relationship? First, you need some vital information. That is, you have to inquire about the offended person's requirements. Along that line, I did some research about forgiveness and healing relationships.

In their book *The Five Languages of Apology*, Dr. Gary Chapman and Dr. Jennifer Thomas identify these five languages:

1. Expressing regret: "I am sorry."
2. Accepting responsibility: "I was wrong."
3. Making restitution: "What can I do to make it right?"
4. Genuinely repenting: "I'll try not to do that again."
5. Requesting forgiveness: "Will you please forgive me?"

The point is that people have different preferences as to what makes a "real apology." For example, when I have discussed this topic with college students in my Comparative Religion class, many of them felt strongly that it is not an apology unless the person says, "I was wrong."

Upon personal reflection, I realized that when a family member apologizes to me, I also have a certain preference. It is related to "genuinely repenting." However, I noticed that the phrase "I'll try not to do that again," leaves me feeling uneasy. My preference is to hear, "Here is my plan so I can avoid doing that again."

Discover the Offended Person's Preferred Language of Apology

At some point, if possible, ask, "Would you please talk about a time when someone apologized in a way that worked for you?"

An interviewer asked me about this, "What if the person is extremely angry? Would he really answer such a question?"

I replied, "It's true. There are times when the offended person will walk away and not even answer; or the offended person will hang up on you if you try to talk with him or her on the telephone. Timing is crucial. Sometimes, it helps to ask this question with a neutral third person present. Maybe a mutual friend."

Trudy saw her friends Calendra and Penny taking a coffee break. Steeling herself, Trudy walked up and said, "Hi, Calendra, Penny." Penny flinched; she was the offended person.

Trudy continued, "This will just take two minutes. Penny, I was wondering (because I want to get back into your good graces) if you might tell me about what makes a real apology to you?"

Penny pointedly turned to Calendra and said, "If you want, you could tell Trudy that a good apology requires that the person say, 'I was wrong.'"

Trudy replied, looking at Penny, "Penny, I know now that I was wrong. And I—"

Penny abruptly got up and walked away. But Trudy felt that she had made a start. She had publicly stated her intention to apologize, and made a good first attempt.

At one point, I was working with a colleague, "George." I did my best to bring up a topic in a gentle way. But he took offense.

I said something like, "You don't need to do a workshop on this title. We could open the possibility of another team member doing the workshop." Frankly, I was stunned with the venom in his response. Apparently, he thought I was being unfair by not setting it up that only he had the first pick of the topics.

At that point, I realized that his intense emotions metaphorically stuffed his ears, so he couldn't hear me. Eventually, I said, "How can I make amends?"

George's response surprised me. He replied, "I don't know how. But thanks for asking." And, here's the good part. His icy demeanor melted and our interactions were positive once again.

This is the power of inquiring.

Principle

Inquire about what the offended person thinks is a good apology.

Power Questions

Are you comfortable asking the question "Would you please talk about a time when someone apologized in a way that worked for you?" Or would another form of question feel better to you? Write down three possibilities.

Tom Marcoux

NURTURE
(#2 of the I.N.F.L.U.E.N.C.E. Process)

To return to someone's good graces, you need to be strong. You need patience and energy. In essence, you must nurture yourself.

Better keep yourself clean and bright; you are the window through which you must see the world. - George Bernard Shaw

Let's face it. You may have made a mistake, but it hurts you that the person is not forgiving you. In fact, you may find yourself to be angry. Say something in anger and you have poured lighter fluid on the flame of the offended person's blazing upset.

We're talking about you becoming strong so that you can influence the person to become calm and eventually let positive feelings rekindle. Throughout this book, an important point is that you influence another person by developing kind, compassionate energy in yourself.

Your Secret Charisma form of influence is this: you nurture yourself so that your positive state of being guides the offended person to soften a hard stance.

So with our discussion of nurturing, we're actually talking about nurturing yourself during this crisis time.

Realize that true happiness lies within you. Waste no time and effort searching for peace and contentment and joy in the world outside. Remember that there is no happiness in having or in getting, but only in giving. Reach out. Share. Smile. Hug. Happiness is a perfume you cannot pour on others without getting a few drops on yourself. - Og Mandino

You become powerful as you realize, as Og suggests, that true happiness lies within you. Happiness is not merely "feeling good." It is a deep knowing of your capabilities. Make yourself capable of withstanding a storm with poise and calm. In my book *Nothing Can Stop You This Year*, I share the nurturing power of the Low Mood First Aid Kit.

My clients have noted these parts of their personal Low Mood First Aid Kit:

- Inspirational book or audio CD
- MP3 player with favorite music (perhaps, an iPod)
- Photo of his or her children
- Photo of himself or herself with romantic partner in a joyful mood at a relaxing place
- Reminders to take a walk outside, soak in a hot bath or call loving friends

It is crucial to have certain activities that you can do on your own to elevate your mood.*

* If you or someone you know has persistent, severe low mood experiences, medical help may be needed. For many people, a combination of medicine and talk-therapy has proved effective for

working with symptoms of clinical depression.

* * *

Method 1: Let a Negative Thought Float Away

My client, Amanda, has a recurring thought that can drain her energy in seconds: "My mother doesn't respect me or my choices. She thinks I'm an idiot." After working with me, Amanda has developed a process in which she just allows that thought to flow away. She treats her thoughts like leaves floating down a stream of water. In fact, she looks for another thought immediately—something uplifting like: "I love the comments of my students. They tell me how I helped them improve their artwork and that I have given them hope to pursue their artistic careers." I call this process the *Floating Leaves Method.*

This process of letting a negative thought float away and then choosing to focus on a positive, uplifting thought can help you live more moments in an empowered way. You'll feel better more of the time!

Method 2: Use Write Down–Rip Up to Handle Anger

Anger can drain us of vital energy that we need to pursue our big dreams. Years ago, when I worked in a particular corporation, a manager said something to me that was so rude, offensive and inappropriate that my internal reaction was intense anger. Fortunately, I had heard about writing down my thoughts to get them out of my system. I added an important twist: I ripped up the page and put it in my pocket. If that manager had found my comments, I would have been shown the door!

By ripping up the page, I also ensured that I did not re-read my comments. I got them out of my system, and the rest of my day was not permanently marred by one person's momentary crass behavior.

You now have a method to empower yourself when someone attempts to cut you down. Make the choice to use the Write Down–Rip Up process, and you will strengthen yourself.

Method 3: Use a Pattern-Interrupt to Shift to a Positive Mood

Often, words are not enough. We need to put our body into action, which will create a ripple effect in our thoughts and feelings.

For example, my client Max uses a lightly closed fist tapped twice on his right thigh to snap out of a negative thought pattern. When he feels tired at work, he taps his closed fist and tells himself: "I can do this. I can do this."

The process of using his body combined with empowering words functions as a Pattern-Interrupt for his previous behaviors. You can choose how to interrupt self-defeating behaviors.

- Identify a self-defeating behavior pattern. Write it in a personal journal.
- Write down two ways to use your body and an empowering idea. (Use a Pattern-Interrupt process to elevate your mood.)

Remember, low moods come and go, but we have choices for how we ride them out. We can take action to help shorten the duration of a low mood.

* * *

If you're not feeling good in this moment, you can use certain sentences to switch the direction of your thoughts. This is crucial because from thoughts come feelings. I call this process: Use a switch-phrase. It's like shifting a rail switch so that a train
gets on a new track and into a new direction.

Quotations when engraved upon the memory give you good thoughts. - Winston Churchill

For example, I have memorized a number of quotes from notable people. Just in an instant, I can recall Eleanor Roosevelt's comment: "Do what you feel in your heart is right—for you will be criticized anyway."
I can use the comment as a guide. And this comment can switch me into an empowering state of being.

Principle
Nurture yourself when you're in a crisis in which an offended person refuses to forgive you.

Power Question
Which Low Mood First Aid Kit method seized your attention? Pull out your day planner or calendar and schedule time to use that method. Take action.

FLEX YOUR OPTIONS
(#3 of the I.N.F.L.U.E.N.C.E. Process)

Imagine that someone you love and care about has abruptly severed all communication. Feels bad, right?

That's what happened to me, and it led to my writing this section to be helpful to you.

As I mentioned earlier, my elderly father cut off communication with me. He would not come to the phone when I called, and he had my mother say, "He's busy." I was aware that, at 71 years old, my father had a limited amount of time remaining on this planet.

He felt he was absolutely right. He had no interest in hearing me or in changing. The healing of the relationship was completely in my hands alone.

He cut off my options. First, no phone calls. Next, he would leave the house if I visited my parents in the city where they live.

This section is about flexing your options. Clearly, I needed to find another option—another way to communicate with my father to express my appreciation of his previous kind and supportive actions.

Expressing Gratitude Can Restore a Relationship

So I found a different way to connect with my father. I sent him a happy-looking card, which depicted Kermit the Frog playing the banjo.

I wrote:

Dad,
Happy today. Thank you for holding me to high standards. This has made my life better.
Love, Tom

This heartfelt comment from me helped my father feel better. Soon we were talking on the phone and meeting in person again.*

* My father and I had a heartfelt conversation, to include this story in this book.

Have the courage to act instead of react.
- Oliver Wendell Holmes

If I had followed my father's unfortunate example, this situation could have turned into a grudge or a feud. The problem with delays when people are feeling bad is that people can become thoroughly entrenched in their own opinion and point of view. It becomes even more painful to loosen up from being so rigid.

Consider this old spiritual phrase: Would you rather be right or happy?

Apparently, when we look around at this world, numerous individuals prefer to be "right"—to the point of war and other horrible outcomes.

Nothing is softer or more flexible than water, yet nothing can resist it. - Lao-tzu

So now, I invite you to flex your options. Pull out a sheet of paper or your personal journal and write down three names of important people in your life. Next to each name, write three ways you could express appreciation for that person (even an unreasonable supervisor, for example).

Give us grace and strength to forbear and to persevere. Give us courage and gaiety and the quiet mind. - Robert Louis Stevenson

Stevenson's comment reminds us that we may need to pray to a Higher Power for help. That is a powerful option!

When I stand before God at the end of my life, I would hope that I would not have a single bit of talent left, and could say, "I used everything You gave me." - Erma Bombeck

So use your imagination and creativity to find ways to communicate appreciation—even when someone has temporarily caused you pain.

Your intention to bring healing to the relationship is primary.

Your best work is not the triumph of technique but the purity of purpose. - Tom Marcoux

Make a Schedule to Take Action

When you really want something, in this case to restore a business or personal relationship, you need a schedule. Not just a goal. An old phrase is a goal without a deadline is just a wish. So you need a schedule.

You have lost the trust of the offended person. You need to rebuild that trust. It takes time—and consistent effort.

I write five pages a day. If you would read five pages a day, we'd stay right even. - Robert Parker

I shared this quote for three reasons: to provide a bit of humor; to show the commitment to daily action; and to remind us about how a relationship works. We note a "doer" and a "receiver." In the case of the quote, we have a writer and a reader.

To restore your relationship, what do you need to do? It comes down to three actions.

Schedule These Three Actions and You Will Go F.A.R.

To make it easy to remember, I refer to the F.A.R. process:

- Forgiveness—ask for forgiveness.
- Amends—seek to make amends.
- Regret—express your regret.

My distinction is that you need to do these actions repeatedly until the person "gives in" and finally says, "Okay. Okay. I forgive you."

Jack forgot to pick up his girlfriend, Sarah, at the train station. She had previously warned him that she was sensitive about "being abandoned." She even told him the story that she had been left at a day-care center on the afternoon when her parents had a big blow-up that culminated in their divorce.

Sarah's grief and anger were so huge that they surprised her. Sarah delivered the "killing blow" by yelling at Jack: "You're just as thoughtless as my father!"

Jack remembered that he wanted to go F.A.R. in his relationship with Sarah so he set up his personal schedule:

- Once a week, ask for forgiveness
- Three times a week, express his regret
- Four times a week, take action to make amends

He not only scheduled these actions into his day planner, but also went even further. To amend his faulty behavior, he purchased a personal digital assistant that would provide him with an alarm to remind him to perform these actions. It took some time but eventually Sarah forgave Jack. She mentioned that his consistent effort helped.

I once read: "A goal is accountable when it's countable."

How to ask for forgiveness

You could say something like: "Our relationship is so important to me. I know I did wrong. It's tearing me up inside that we're not close. Would you please forgive me?"

A number of people need significant time to get to the place of forgiveness. They might even say, "I want to forgive you, but I ... but I can't now—not yet." So you need to maintain your own patience and continue to consistently follow through with F.A.R.—ask for forgiveness; make amends; and express regret.

By the way, for me, if a family member hurts me, what counts to me is to hear his or her plan on how the mistake will not happen again. That is big part of making amends to me.

Just keep taking action and realize:

All difficult things have their origin in that which is easy, and great things in that which is small.
- Lao-tzu

Your small steps add up to melting the offended person's heart.

Nature does not hurry, yet everything is accomplished.
- Lao-tzu

Principle

You truly flex your options when you schedule the actions to restore the relationship.

Power Questions

How are you going to schedule the F.A.R. process? That is, what specific times will you: ask for forgiveness; make amends; and express your regret?

LISTEN
(#4 of the I.N.F.L.U.E.N.C.E. Process)

What is crucial for you to restore a relationship? Listening. Let's face it, the offended person wants to bend your ear over and over again, to ensure that you hear exactly what you did wrong and the hurt you caused.

It is up to you to make it easier for the person to tell how his or her heart is in agony.

When we are listened to, it creates us, makes us unfold and expand. Ideas actually begin to grow within us and come to life.
- Brenda Ueland

It helps if, at appropriate times, you say something like:
- I know I was wrong. I'm really upset that I hurt you. Do you want to tell me what trouble my mistake caused you?
- I can hear how hurt you've been feeling. Do you want to tell me more?

After the offended person has expressed his or her feelings for a time, it may seem that the person has run out of gas. However, to really facilitate healing it is often better for us to ask: "Is there anything else?" You'll be surprised at what comes up next. A friend told me how she listens, sometimes for two hours, to a roommate until the roommate "runs out of gas." Then her roommate is okay.

Dr. John Gray talks about how men make the mistake of trying to block their female romantic partner from "hitting bottom." When you listen to the offended person, you are allowing the person to hit bottom and take you with him or her!

At that point, it is like the offended person is yelling: "See! See what damage you caused! You should feel bad about this!"

Courage is found in unlikely places. - J.R.R. Tolkien

It takes courage and strength to listen to an offended person. But only through listening will you help the person feel heard and respected.

Use Reflective Replies

A powerful part of listening is expressing Reflective Replies. This is the process of providing a metaphorical mirror so that the person knows that you really heard him or her. Here are examples:
- That sounds like that was frustrating …
- That sounds like it upset the whole thing. How could you go on from there?

Your first step to healing your relationship after you have made a big mistake is for you to devote significant time to listening.

Samantha was surprised when her business partner, Dave, rushed into the office and shouted, "You were supposed to carry the ball while I was in New York!" At that point, Samantha found it helpful to listen to Dave without offering defensive comments. After Dave cooled off, they worked together to come up with a new plan that better reflected their different talents and inclinations.

Listening is powerful.

Principle
When you're listening, you help the person drain off his or her feelings of being offended.

Power Question
How can you take care of yourself so that you are strong enough to listen to the offended person's anger and restrain yourself from making defensive replies?

UNDERSTAND
(#5 of the I.N.F.L.U.E.N.C.E. Process)

When can understanding a situation help you heal a disrupted relationship? When you can reduce the intensity of your own feelings.

For example, imagine you're in a restaurant. The waiter slams your dish on the table in front of you and the way he plunks down your utensils gets on your nerves. It's easy to think, "What a jerk! He doesn't care about being kind and helpful. He should get another job!"

But now imagine that you know that three minutes ago he received a phone call confirming that his young son has leukemia. If you understood this, wouldn't that cool down your anger?

I hear and I forget. I see and I remember. I do and I understand.
- Confucius

What do you do? You take a moment to imagine how your mistake may have caused big, painful feelings in the offended person. This use of your imagination can help you be more patient as the offended person expresses negative feelings.

You don't develop courage by being happy in your relationships every day. You develop it by surviving difficult times and challenging adversity. - Epicurus

All the great things are simple, and many can be expressed in a single word: freedom, justice, honor, duty, mercy, hope.
- Winston Churchill

You must hold the hope for reconciliation for the relationship. The offended person does not have the strength or vision. You must hold the vision.

Because you made the mistake, it is your duty to the relationship to be patient. You need to let go of your preference that the offended person hurry up and forgive you already! To get to the point of forgiving you, the offended person must go through his or her own personal grief process.

In essence, you do your duty by taking action to express the three elements of F.A.R. Our earlier example included:

- Once a week, ask for forgiveness
- Three times a week, express regret
- Four times a week, take action to make amends

To make the best of the process of *Your Secret Charisma*, you need to get clear in your own heart. What do you truly want? To restore the relationship? Then, you need to step forward with courage, kindness and persistence.

It took me four years of consistent effort to help one of my most treasured friendships heal after a bumpy time when a business project failed. Through my efforts and the responses of my friend, our friendship flowed onward.

To Inspire Forgiveness, Give Forgiveness

I once heard a speaker say that the fastest way to experience something is to give another person the experience of it. You want forgiveness to be granted to you from the offended person, then you need to forgive the offended person. What? Yes, you need to forgive the offended person for not granting you forgiveness immediately. Isn't the offended person hurting you because he or she has not said, "That's okay. You're normally a kind and trustworthy person. This is unlike you. You're forgiven"?

You will never change things by fighting the existing reality. To change something, build a new model that makes the existing model obsolete. - R. Buckminster Fuller

You need to be the model of forgiveness. And in *Chapter Two, To Influence, You Must Have Energy, Poise and Charisma,* we will cover techniques so that you get stronger.

Here, I want to emphasize that enhancing your understanding can assist you in making better decisions. You'll decide to give the other person a break. You'll restrain yourself from saying unkind words when you feel irritated. You'll make consistent efforts to demonstrate your concern and desire for the relationship to heal.

Principle
Enhance your understanding, and it is easier for you to be patient and to restrain from expressing negative reactions.

Power Questions

Can you imagine the hurt feelings your mistake caused for the offended person? Does this help you give the other person a break? Can you set aside your preference that the person forgive you quickly? And can you keep "doing your duty" and continue your F.A.R. efforts?

ENERGIZE
(#6 of the I.N.F.L.U.E.N.C.E. Process)

Have you heard someone or yourself say, "When I have the energy I'll try that"? The truth is that we often find energy when we take effective action. The energy arises as you experience doing the appropriate actions.

There is no way to happiness. Happiness is the way.
- Dr. Wayne Dyer

Have you noticed that if you smile, you feel better? Researchers have noted that merely putting a pen in a test-subject's mouth (which approximates a smile) actually helps people feel better!

So the question is, what are these good and appropriate actions?

In this chapter, we will identify what works in two situations:
- Enhancing your romantic relationship
- Enhancing a business relationship

Enhancing your romantic relationship

Are you ready for some profound information that can greatly increase the daily happiness that you and your romantic partner experience?

Here it is: Dr. Gary Chapman communicates profound strategies in his bestselling book *The Five Love Languages.*

Here are the five primary love languages:

1. Words of affirmation
2. Acts of service
3. Receiving gifts
4. Quality time
5. Physical touch

At the beginning of courtship, we drop everything and throw all kinds of loving actions into the mix. In that way, we're bound to, by accident, provide the loving kindness in the way our partner needs.

So how does this relate to getting out of trouble—that is, healing your relationship—if your partner feels offended?

We need to pay close attention to our partner to discover his or her primary love language.

The tough part is that after you have been a romantic couple for a while, then you return to your standard, busy, daily life. And that preoccupation with daily busyness causes our loved one to starve for love!

An interviewer asked me, "Why?"

I replied, "Just to survive in this fast-paced modern world, we often give all our energy away at the office. We leave the remaining crumbs for our partner."

Make Every Loving Gesture You Do Really Count!

We don't have extra time to be flailing about—guessing, failing, getting frustrated and angry.

When you learn your loved one's primary love language—and you speak it well—you will save a lot of time that was formerly lost to misunderstandings. We lose time and energy when we're torn up inside because of misunderstandings.

Now, I'll give you some examples of how my clients have expressed love via the five love languages:

Words of affirmation

You hold her hands and look her in the eyes and say, "Honey, I really appreciated how you listened to all my new business ideas. It means so much to me because I really treasure your insight. I know it took a lot of effort for you. I know you really love me."

In your personal journal, write down your own version of words of affirmation.

Acts of service

You ask your loved one, "What can I do that would help you feel really loved by me?"

Women like delightful surprises. Yes, my sweetheart tells me that all the time.

For example, Matthew washed the dishes so that his wife returned home to a cleaned kitchen.

In your personal journal, write down your own version of acts of service. By the way, ask your partner. Often what we think is a great service is something that is not even on our partner's radar screen. So "do unto your partner as she would prefer done unto her."

Receiving gifts

Throughout the year, listen carefully for what your loved one says he or she would love to see or own. If she says, "I just love flowers!" you have received your marching orders. If he says, "Oh, if only I had a Craftsman power tool, I could make my cabinet really sturdy," you have an idea for a helpful gift.

Also, think of providing gifts on days other than your partner's birthday, Valentine's Day or the Holiday season. I provide a gift and write, "Happy Today!"

In your personal journal, write down your own version of receiving gifts.

Quality time

About quality time, Dr. Gary Chapman writes, "Giving another person your undivided attention communicates, 'You are important to me.' Quality time means no distractions. The TV is off … ."

For example, my client Harry had to learn that his wife had different feelings when he talked about his latest project. Although Harry felt he was talking from his heart, his wife heard something else: "Here we go again. Harry's talking about work." Even though Harry puts his heart into his work (his own business), his wife considers quality time to be talking together about something else. And quality time is about listening to your loved one.

In your personal journal, write down your own version of quality time.

Physical touch

Many hard-charging men only allow themselves to be nurtured and protected in their loved one's arms. Researchers report that many women find it difficult to be touched or to reach out with loving touches when they feel hurt. It becomes a burning bridge that cannot be crossed, until one of the partners reaches out with courage and extra effort. This is precisely the reason that learning each other's primary love language is crucial. Without the goodwill created by speaking your love partner's love language, there is no foundation or energy to reach out to each other.

To make life even more complicated, researchers show that often:

- Men don't feel loved without sexual intimacy
- Women don't feel capable of sexual intimacy without emotional intimacy/closeness happening before any possible sexual intimacy

Keep physical touch happening throughout your days, include holding hands and hugging.

Writing about hugging, Dr. David Schnarch, in his book *Passionate Marriage,* introduces a crucial, powerful technique that he calls *hugging until relaxed*. The idea is to embrace each other while standing on your own two feet—both literally and metaphorically. Dr. Schnarch writes,

"The basics require four sentences: Stand on your own two feet. Put your arms around your partner. Focus on yourself. Quiet yourself down—way down."

This is a process that takes practice. I know this from

personal experience. My mind moves fast and when I'm working I move fast. It is important for me to practice making a transition to a relaxed state of being.

In your personal journal, write down your own version of physical touch.

* * *

Enhance a Business Relationship

We have been talking about actions that create positive, life-enhancing energy—both your own energy and that of the other person.

Here is a big energy drain in a business relationship: notice how people make snap judgments and become offended when someone fails to express appropriate gratitude. Suddenly, all the positive energy that was building in the relationship has been drained away.

The problem is each individual has different requirements for what feels like a good expression of gratitude.

As mentioned earlier, Gary Chapman points out that each person has a personal "love language." If you speak the person's language, he or she will truly experience your gratitude. (This is something that I talk about in my book *Be Heard and Be Trusted: How You Can Use Secrets of the Greatest Communicators to Get What You Want*.)

The five love languages
1. Words of affirmation
2. Receiving gifts
3. Acts of service
4. Quality time
5. Physical touch

Our goal is to appropriately and effectively express gratitude and create positive feelings.

You want to express your gratitude in a way that the person can readily accept and feel.

Now, I'll provide examples of how you can appropriately express gratitude when working with a colleague or customer.

Words of affirmation

"Joe, thanks for all your efforts. You were really effective in finding solutions so that our two teams could work together. Thank you."

Receiving gifts

A small, appropriate gift that relates to the person's hobby can be helpful. It's great when we honor people. Many businesses honor long-time customers with coupons for discounted products or services.

Acts of service

Often, a customer will appreciate receiving an article that relates to the hobby of her son or daughter. In this way, you can enrich your business relationship with the customer. The idea of service is that you extend an extra effort for the other person's well-being.

Quality time

When meeting with a new customer, turn off your cell phone. When someone stops talking to us, and places accepting a cell phone call above us, it hurts. Don't let that happen with your new customer.

Physical touch

Each person needs to be careful about physically touching a customer. If the new customer had earlier extended his or her hand for a good handshake, then you can shake hands as part of expressing gratitude. However, some people, such as Donald Trump, do not like to shake hands. In that case, you can nod and smile.

* * *

In summary, we have talked about ways to create positive energy. In a personal relationship, express your love in the appropriate love language. In a business relationship, express gratitude in a way that the other person can readily accept and feel good about. And if you are working with people from different cultures, read a book* and attend workshops to learn the appropriate etiquette.

* My book *Be Heard and Be Trusted* covers a number of details about how to interact with people of different cultures.

Principle
To create positive energy in a relationship, express your good intentions according to the "language" the other person readily takes in.

Power Question
In talking with your loved one, would you feel comfortable asking, "Remember the last time you felt totally

loved, what happened?" In a business relationship, listen carefully to the customer's comments. Notice if she says that another business really showed her that they appreciated her business. Notice what brings light to her eyes. Find a way to express your appreciation in an appropriate and similar manner.

NEGOTIATE
(#7 of the I.N.F.L.U.E.N.C.E. Process)

What is one of the hardest questions to ask in the process of healing a personal or business relationship? I have noticed that people hesitate to ask, "How can I make amends?"

One reason clients have given me for why they hesitate is due to the fear that the offended person will ask for too much. In this section, I'll show you how to negotiate so that you can regain the trust of the offended person.

Negotiate for time to consider what you will agree to

The American Heritage Dictionary defines negotiate as "to arrange or settle by discussion and mutual agreement." Now, that definition avoids the distasteful baggage that a number of people put on the term negotiate.

Donald Trump is a person with fans and detractors, but many people do acknowledge his negotiating skills. He described his ten negotiating tips:

"1. Know exactly what you want, and focus on that.

2. View any conflict as an opportunity. This will expand your mind as well as your horizons.

3. Know that your negotiating partner may well have exactly the same goals as you do. Do not underestimate them.

4. Patience is an enormous virtue and needs to be cultivated for successful negotiation on any level.

5. Realize that quiet persistence can go a long way. Being stubborn is often an attribute. The key is to know when to loosen up.

6. Remain optimistic at all times. Practice positive thinking.

7. Let your guard down, but only on purpose. Watch how your negotiating partners respond.

8. Be open to change—it's another word for innovation.

9. Trust your instincts, even after you've honed your skills. They're there for a reason.

10. Negotiation is an art. Treat it like one."

When you want to exert secret influence to get you out of trouble, you can use a number of the above tips. And now, I'll show you a powerful method: gaining think-space.

Avoid fear and gain *think-space*

You do not need to fear the offended person's response to your question, "How can I make amends?" The important detail is to be ready to respond appropriately to gain *think-space*. Think-space is my term for having both time and an expanse so that you can carefully consider a request. Sometimes, a person can become a people-pleaser and say yes too quickly.

Make sure to express your concern and desire to heal the relationship. You ask: "How can I make amends?" And after the offended person responds, you can say:

"I'm glad that you told me that. I'm interested in doing what will help us take care of the mistake I made and for us to feel closer again. Let me think about this overnight. I'm not sure how I can do what you're talking about. But I'm going to really look into it."

In a business transaction, you can replace "feel closer again" with something like:

"I'm interested in doing what will help us take care of the mistake so that you feel good about moving forward with our first plan."

What to do in your next conversation

When you have your next conversation after the offended person has stated her "demands," it is important to begin with what you can do. A reply can be like Steve's comment to his wife:

"Janet, I have thought carefully about what you said. First, I'm glad to tell you that I can take the kids on Tuesday and Thursday nights so that you are free to attend the classes you mentioned. I can also do the laundry first thing on Saturday mornings. I'll still need to look into the Sunday thing. At this moment, I feel I'd better hold on to my Sunday afternoon bike ride. In fact, I think I made my mistake because I let myself get upside-down and too stressed out. So let me make a good start with Tuesdays and Thursdays. And we'll keep talking, okay?"

When Steve says this, he includes the following strategies:

He makes sure that Janet knows she is winning

"Janet, I have thought carefully about what you said. First, I'm glad to tell you that I can take the kids on Tuesday and Thursday nights so that you are free to attend the classes you mentioned. I can also do the laundry first thing on Saturday mornings."

He does not over-promise

"I'll still need to look into the Sunday thing. At this moment, I feel I'd better hold onto my Sunday afternoon bike ride. In fact, I think I made my mistake because I let myself get upside-down and too stressed out."

He ends with the positive news

"So let me make a good start with Tuesdays and Thursdays."

He demonstrates that he wants to care for her needs

"And we'll keep talking, okay?"

To me, there is no greater act of courage than being the one who kisses first. - Janeane Garofalo

By agreeing to take action and by holding his ground about the Sunday bike rides, Steve is demonstrating love and courage.

The softest things in the world overcome the hardest things in the world. - Lao-tzu

In this quote Lao-tzu is referring to water, which over the years can create something as impressive as the Grand Canyon. Similarly, once you ask, "How can I make amends?" and you start negotiating solutions, you can overcome a hardened heart.

Principle
Ask how you can make amends, gain think-space and realistically negotiate how you can take positive action in a helpful direction.

Power Question
How can you ask for think-space? Consider something like: "I've listened carefully. I'm going to need to see how I can make this happen. How about we talk about it tomorrow afternoon?"

CREATE (NOT COMPETE)
(#8 of the I.N.F.L.U.E.N.C.E. Process)

What do you do when someone is offended and you did nothing wrong?

We discover that the first thing we need to do is put our ego in check.

When I was young, I observed that nine out of ten things I did were failures. So I did ten times more work.
- George Bernard Shaw

We might say that it is "work" to restrain ourselves from expressing our impatience. Often, an offended person seems to forget every kind word or action that we have done for years! Pain is powerful. It can fill the offended person's world until they cannot see past it.

So we're left with doing "ten times more work." Often, since we have caused the damage, we must undo what we have created. And, there are times when the other person has misinterpreted something and we need to continue to be kind to the offended person until he or she can view things with more insight.

When you are content to be simply yourself and don't compare or compete, everybody will respect you. - Lao-tzu

So we must not "compete" or compare ourselves and our previous patience with the offended person's current "unreasonableness."

What we must do is create opportunities to show kindness to the offended person. As I mentioned in the prior chapter, we ask, "How can I make amends?" and then we get busy.

Kindness in words creates confidence. Kindness in thinking creates profoundness. Kindness in giving creates love. - Lao-tzu

A number of spiritual authors emphasize, "Would you rather be right or happy?"

So now that we have made a mistake, we must remind ourselves: "What I really want is healing for this relationship."

Keep on the lookout for ways to show that you care. Send a little gift. If you are rebuffed, try again in two weeks. If necessary, make a kind gesture once a month.

We never know what will happen next. Perhaps sometime in the future, the offended person suffers a big disappointment or even a loss of a loved one. Who is there to provide comfort? You are.

Someone made a comment to me that had a lasting impact: "When my mother died, my friends disappeared."

Many people will disappear because they don't know how to handle the situation.

But you, who are acting like a hero to restore the relationship, can call and gently ask, "Is there something I can help with?"

Principle
If you feel the offended person is not as kind or forgiving as you are, shift your thoughts. Focus on how you can create opportunities to demonstrate your concern and kindness toward the person.

Power Questions
Are you feeling slighted by the offended person's forgetfulness of how you have been trustworthy in the past? Shift your thoughts to how you can create opportunities to be kind and helpful. What are the offended person's concerns? Can you provide a helpful article sent via mail (yes, snail mail with a hand-written note)? Can you send a soothing card or, perhaps, a CD of soothing music?

Tom Marcoux

EMBRACE
(#9 of the I.N.F.L.U.E.N.C.E. Process)

Be like water making its way through cracks ... You put water into a bottle and it becomes the bottle. You put it in a teapot; it becomes the teapot. Now, water can flow or it can crash. Be water, my friend. - Bruce Lee

In order to get into the good graces of someone you offended, you need to be like water. And you need to embrace the process. When you ask someone, Will you forgive me? the offended person has the right to reply, "No. Not yet." You also need to embrace your own feelings about this. You might be feeling terrible, and have thoughts like: "How dare he not give me a break this time! After all the times I have forgiven him!"

To love means loving the unlovable. To forgive means pardoning the unpardonable. Faith means believing the unbelievable. Hope means hoping when everything seems hopeless. - G. K. Chesterton

You're going to need to embrace yourself. You need to nurture yourself. If your partner has withdrawn from you, then you are now grieving and in pain. You must gain support from other sources. Perhaps seeing a counselor will provide you with the essential support you need during this crisis time.

One man with courage makes a majority. - Andrew Jackson

When I talk about embrace, I am emphasizing that you need to embrace your new role. You are now the healer of the relationship. You are the only one whom you can count on to do what is necessary to guide the relationship forward—after taking enough time to acknowledge the hurt you created.

You become the "one person who makes a majority." You will provide the spiritual leadership for the relationship.

I know this is true because I have had to take on this role. For example, at one point I did something that I felt was right for my family, but it caused great inconvenience to a friend. So I had to keep calling that friend once a month for two years to seek to restore the relationship. This friend was being guided by his family members to "write me off." I knew in my heart that if I did not keep up the effort, that friend would just disappear. Now, both my friend and I are glad about my persistence.

A spiritual idea holds that, in a relationship, the person who is more "sane" at the time needs to take care of the relationship. It may seem to be a stretch to say that the offended person is not completely sane. But have you heard about people being "blinded by anger"? The truth is that someone who is blinded by anger or pain does not have access to his or her full senses. The offended person cannot remember all of the times that you have proven trustworthy. So not only must you remain consistent in showing your concern and kindness, but you must do even more.

So embrace your new role, gain the support you need and persist like the hero you are now becoming.

Principle
Embrace your new role in providing spiritual leadership to the relationship—and be sure to nurture yourself along the way.

Power Questions
What have you lost now that the offended person has shut you out? Can you go to family members, friends and/or a counselor to gain the support you need to remain strong, kind and persistent?

CONCLUSION TO CHAPTER ONE

In Chapter One, we have explored the I.N.F.L.U.E.N.C.E. process:

I – Inquire
N – Nurture
F – Flex your options
L – Listen
U – Understand
E – Energize
N – Negotiate
C – Create (not compete)

E – Embrace

We realize that the secret influence to get you out of trouble is mainly about becoming stronger and being in a calm state for yourself.

Your Secret Charisma form of influence is how your calm state of being can transfer to the offended person and soften a hardened attitude.
You must provide spiritual leadership to yourself and to the offended person so that healing can take place.

Your secret influence includes specific methods of asking questions to help the person express her pain and then to show how you have truly heard her.

In the section on "embrace," we looked at possible sources of support. This process is so crucial that in *Chapter Two, To Influence, You Must Have Energy, Poise and Charisma*, we will cover essential methods so you can enhance your own healing.

Let's move forward …

CHAPTER TWO:
INFLUENCE THROUGH ENERGY, POISE, AND CHARISMA
(HOW TO HEAL WHEN LIFE'S TOO MUCH)

In Chapter One, you learned specific methods of asking questions so that you can demonstrate your sincerity with the offended person.

In Chapter Two, you will learn the heart of the Secret Influence Process. You must become stronger and maintain a calm state of being. This is when you radiate Your Secret Charisma. Then your kind and calm state of being can ultimately transfer to the offended person. She or he will become free to let go of the pain and then join with you in moving the relationship forward. This ability to remain calm helps you be at your best during the any moment that is crucial to an interaction.

As I mentioned earlier, the Secret Influence Process includes the following:
- Strengthen yourself
- Remain in a calm state of being

- Communicate your concern and kindness
- Take action with the F.A.R. methods (forgiveness, amends, regret)

Chapter Two focuses on:

- Strengthening yourself; and
- Remaining in a calm state of being.

Being deeply loved by someone gives you strength; loving someone deeply gives you courage. - Lao-tzu

When you have offended a loved one, you have just lost a major source of strength. With your loved one holding you at arm's length, you have suffered a loss. You are now grieving. So now you need to learn *How to Heal When Life's Too Much*.

The idea of *How to Heal When Life's Too Much* began when I slept every night at the Sequoia Hospital to be with my sweetheart who was at death's door. And while commuting to see her in the hospital, I was rear-ended by a commercial truck. My injury sent me to Stanford Medical Center.

At that point, one idea filled my mind: *How to Heal When Life's Too Much*. At that time, with my sweetheart in the hospital and with me in another hospital, I truly felt overwhelmed.

Some days later, my train derailed as it arrived in San Francisco. I joked with friends, "I'm not getting on a plane this month!"

In order to strengthen yourself, you need to engage in the process of healing on a moment-to-moment basis.

We use the H.E.A.L. process:

H – Humor
E – Energize
A – Act
L – Listen

Let's take the next steps ...

HUMOR
(#1 of the H.E.A.L. Process)

Sometimes, we hear, "Well, just humor him. Let him say what he needs to say." We profoundly affect our lives when we listen to our physical and emotion pains. We humor them; that is, we accept them. We say, "Okay, illness I hear you. Hmmm, I imagine you're telling me to slow down."

As I mentioned, I found myself at Stanford Medical Center after being rear-ended by a commercial truck. My attention was seized at the beginning of physical rehabilitation. As the physical therapist manipulated my injured neck area, I felt great sadness and discomfort. I felt quite vulnerable. I could have resisted this. Instead, I paused to experience the situation and told her, "I'm feeling kind of … vulnerable. Like I was a 20-year-old who woke up in a 90-year-old body."

In this way, I "humored" the messages of my body and my life. I listened. I did slow down, and I asked my sweetheart's family to help cover more shifts at the hospital. I listened to my body by viewing the physical therapy and personal exercise sessions as my time to focus on my needs and my body.

People who keep stiff upper lips find that it's damn hard to smile. - Judith Guest

Humor and laughter are also lifesavers. Norman Cousins, bestselling author of *Anatomy of an Illness*, was diagnosed with an incurable, life-threatening illness. He found that 15 minutes of laughter gave him two hours of pain-free sleep. His program, which led to his full recovery, included watching films of Laurel and Hardy, Abbott and Costello and the Marx Brothers.

Similarly, it helps if you create comfort and joy for yourself. Enjoy opportunities to laugh through interacting with friends and viewing films.

We don't laugh because we're happy; we're happy because we laugh. - William James

One of my clients found that he brightened his life by making time at the end of his work day to watch a half-hour television show called *Whose Line Is It Anyway?* He set his digital video recorder to record episodes. This was an essential ritual just as valuable as regular exercise sessions. Some people have called laughter "inner jogging."

Emergency medical personnel know the value of "gallows humor" or dark humor to relieve tension. My point is that if any humor occurs, just welcome it and let it flow. Each day is a lifetime, and we welcome the good moments and we handle the bad ones.

Why should we think upon things that are lovely? Because thinking determines life. - William James

Principle
Learn to create more acceptance and humor in your daily life.

Power Question
How can you experience humor on a daily basis?

Tom Marcoux

ENERGIZE
(#2 of the H.E.A.L. Process)

How can we can energize ourselves? First, pause and notice if you have you given up on a personal dream. You can reconnect with your dream. Such reconnection can create a wellspring of personal energy.

Many times, your spirit leads your body. Imagine a time when you faced doing the dishes, and then a family member suggested seeing a movie at the theater. Suddenly, energy coursed through your veins. And you did the dishes in record time!

Similarly, my clients have devoted just 15 minutes to a hobby and found that their whole day was brightened. Additionally, good nutrition and exercise help you expand your personal energy.

A primary source of energy is found in the process of *replace fear with love*. For example, when my sweetheart was in the operating room, I turned my tears and fears into a song of positive prayer—which I played and sang for her after she regained consciousness following the surgery.

When you're serious about recovering your energy you learn powerful coping behaviors.

When the tragedies of September 11, 2001 occurred, many people feared that additional terrorist strikes would occur in more U.S. cities. Immediately, my team and I responded by providing information and presentations to help people cope with the immense stress.

At that point, I pulled together research and spoke to audiences about the C.O.P.E. process. I include that process here because personal and natural disasters occur at various times.

Using the C.O.P.E. process guards your energy. Remember, you need positive, calm energy to exert secret influence. (Again, the following tips were those I presented in the period following the September 11th tragedies.)

C – create time-pockets
O – open to what is unchangeable
P – prepare your options
E – expect and focus on the good

Create—Create time-pockets

Take time to create a little peace for yourself. Don't leave CNN on constantly; maybe check in every two hours (if you're checking on a disaster). Keeping CNN on constantly keeps you in an adrenaline state. When the adrenal glands function too much, you can be vulnerable to health problems. During recent wars, people left CNN on all the time and suffered greatly. Take time to exercise. Make time to read spiritual books. Devote time to talking with family members with the TV off. We need to express our feelings. See a counselor if you feel in distress. Gather in support groups. Make some times when you distract your mind. Seeing a movie can be just the release some people need. Maintain as much of your daily routine as possible.

Open—Open to what is unchangeable

You are a spirit having a human experience. Whatever spiritual practices appeal to you, devote time to them now. Some people feel too stressed to engage in meditation at this time. But the answer is to still to turn off the TV or radio, and take some quiet time for yourself. Write in a journal. Attend a spiritual workshop or devote time in nature. Read spiritual books to gain a larger perspective.

Prepare—Prepare your options

To handle fear, make a list of options. Call an out-of-state friend/family member and set up a place so that family members can call and leave/pick up messages. Talk with friends, get more perspectives and more ideas.

Expect—Expect and focus on the good

We need to release our fear and stress during a tough time. We need to direct our own thoughts in positive directions. This is called Expectation Management. Focus on these thoughts and expectations:
- There is room for hope.
- In this moment, I am all right.
- I can handle this.
- I can learn what I need to do.
- We'll get through this together.
- Things will settle down eventually.

***

Learn to Replace Worry

Many people connect being a good person with worrying about other people. It is important to consider that a replacement for worry is being concerned, taking action (preparing) and letting go. Researchers note that unrelieved stress can cause health problems. It is crucial that everyone becomes conscious of having a coping strategy.

To use the C.O.P.E methods is to form a pattern of supportive habits for your healing.

Habit is stronger than reason. - George Santayana

All things are difficult before they are easy. - Thomas Fuller

Thomas Fuller's quote reminds us that when we start doing new actions they can feel awkward and hard to do. Eventually, we can find that the new healthy habits feel natural. It takes time and practice.

I hear and I forget. I see and I remember. I do and I understand.
- Confucius

Be sure to support your personal energy; develop habits that give you times of refreshment and renewal. Then, you'll have the energy and patience to sincerely listen to the offended person.

Principle
To heal, create more personal energy.

Power Questions

How can you support your personal energy? What are people or situations that drain your energy (energy-drainers)? How can you eliminate or reduce exposure time to energy-drainers?

Tom Marcoux

ACT
(#3 of the H.E.A.L. Process)

Do you ever feel so tired that you long for a time with no fear and no worries? The solution is to function well even when fear is present.

To practice the secret influence to get you out of trouble is to take action to strengthen yourself. Not only do you have the usual bumpy road, but now you're dealing with the added pressure of the offended person's wrath. So we'll now focus on empowering actions you can implement.

I have not ceased being fearful, but I have ceased letting fear control me. - Erica Jong

The idea is to avoid letting the fear of rejection paralyze you from attempting to contact the offended person. Take appropriate action.

Wisdom, compassion, and courage are the three universally recognized moral qualities of [people]. - Confucius

So what kind of actions do you take to rebuild your relationship with the offended person? You have your actions aligned with wisdom, compassion and courage.

Do the thing you fear and the death of fear is certain.
- Ralph Waldo Emerson

Feel the fear and do it anyway. - Susan Jeffers

Identify what you really want and take a step toward it. So if you want the offended person to remember how thoughtful you are, be sure to send a card or gift on important days, such as birthdays and anniversaries. And create an important occasion, such as celebrating some accomplishment that the offended person did months or years ago. You can show how you remember the person's successful efforts. Your card can read, "Happy Two-Year Anniversary for Getting Your First Manuscript Written!"

An interviewer asked, "Is this process of celebrating someone's accomplishment appropriate for business?"

"Yes!" I replied. For example, some years ago, author Dottie Walters told me about how she sent a clipping of an article and congratulated a prospective customer for his recent promotion.

The newly promoted man said to Dottie, "You were the only one who noticed." So we must remember that developing a business relationship involves paying attention and acknowledging people's accomplishments.

Also, take action to nurture and care for yourself. Answer this question: How can I take better care of myself now? Then, note your answer and take a step towards nurturing yourself. Find the support you need. Many clients complain to therapists, "My mother doesn't … [or] my sister doesn't

... " Therapists respond, "What? Were you expecting her to do something different? Were you expecting her to change? Who else can give you the support you need?"

A major act towards healing is to say no graciously and effectively. Learning to say no paves the way so you can say yes to something else. Often it helps to say, "Oh, I'll have to say, 'No, thank you,' at this time. My plate is full. How about I help you brainstorm about someone who can help you with that?"

Another healing action is to use music for relaxation or inspiration. As I type this, I am listening to the music soundtrack of the Indiana Jones movie *Raiders of the Lost Ark*. The love theme is playing, and I feel at peace. Soon, I will feel the surge of energy provided by the heroic theme. Remember, your subconscious mind is listening at every moment. When I hear the heroic theme of Indiana Jones, I feel heroic, strong and capable.

Principle
Press on despite fear and take appropriate action to demonstrate your care and concern for the offended person.

Power Questions
How can you show your care and concern for the offended person? Can you send a postcard or gift to celebrate the bright moments of the person's life?

LISTEN
(#4 of the H.E.A.L. Process)

Who do you wish would really listen to you? Probably one of the first people you thought of was the offended person (if you're reading this book during a difficult time).

Sometimes, when a crucial person is not listening to us, our solution is to listen to ourselves and the lessons of life. Listening is vital to understand life's lessons for us. An old phrase holds, "Life's lessons are repeated in different forms until we learn them." Listen to your body. Does it crave rest? Give it what it needs. Become an expert on healing yourself. If you have some affliction, do some research on the Internet. But remember that statistics can be misused. If a traditional doctor says, "Only two percent of people recover from this," consider that you may be able to nurture yourself and join that two percent.

Realize that, spiritually speaking, we really don't know what a particular illness means in our life—or in the lives of others. That's why I emphasize a concept I call healthy humility.

Healthy humility means to realize that our perceptions may be limited in the moment and that Higher Power may have a greater good in mind.

When my sweetheart was at death's door in the hospital, she experienced an incredible outpouring of love from friends and family members. She soon recovered from major surgery. Certainly, losing an organ was not her preference. But she said, "I didn't know that my friends care so much about me."

We can learn so much by flowing with life as it comes. During the times when I was forced to slow down due to an illness, I have discovered opportunities to grow in empathy with others who face physical challenges.

* * *

Life's Lessons & Experiencing Spiritual Awakening

A special form of listening is the process I refer to as the Divine Aha! When you are reeling from the pain of having someone you love unable to forgive you, it becomes essential for you to listen more—to yourself, the other person and life.

In some moments of life, our soul awakens. We call this the Divine Aha! as in "Aha! Now I get it." Here are useful methods for these moments:

- Be okay with pain that lights your way to the Divine Aha!
- Talk about what you're learning
- Write about what you're learning
- Be gentle with yourself

Accept Pain that Lights Your Way to the Divine Aha!

Sometimes, pain is what grabs our attention. I want to support you to exercise the real freedom that you have. You have the freedom to find your part in any situation that bothers you. Responsibility is really the ability to respond. Responding is choosing rather than reacting (as if by reflex).

To illustrate how pain can light our way to a Divine Aha!, I'll share an example from the world of speaking. When I speak to audiences, I give my loving energy. Many people have written to me about the value, compassion and laughter they've received and enjoyed. But the Divine Aha! arrived in my life when a certain unfavorable critique shook me up.

I had been invited to give a presentation about making books and audio programs. However, the particular critical review showed that the reviewer was not letting my new ideas mix in with his current perceptions. He also included negative comments from two colleagues.

But if I would just pause, I could learn something from this painful review. On the surface, I had been called to teach people how to take action so they could add products to their income-generating activities. But the truth is that many of these audience members were in pain. I realized this when I remembered their comments were about the fear of making mistakes with their first products.

A number of audience members needed me to metaphorically hold their hand. They needed me to acknowledge fears and concerns. If I merely provided a quick answer like, "The easy way to do this is ... " then I was not acknowledging their current situation.

The pain of reading this particular critique led me to look for new ways to interact with audience members. I learned that during a presentation, it's helpful to slow down, perhaps, sit in a chair for a moment or two, and talk quietly with the audience. When addressing an audience that seems edgy, I can say:

"Let's pause for a moment. That last idea seems to have been unusual. It may bring up some questions, or resistance, or even some fears. And I can relate to that. I started off as a painfully shy boy, playing the piano for seniors in a retirement home. I was deeply afraid. My leg was shaking so badly, I was afraid that it would fall off the sustain pedal and make a big thud sound. So now, we're talking about trying a couple of new actions.

And we're here together. Let's talk about it. Who has the first question?"

To illustrate the discomfort of trying new things, I can introduce a physical process of having people fold their hands. People tend to favor putting one thumb over the other. They find that switching positions and placing the other thumb on top to be uncomfortable. The idea is that the audience members experience the discomfort of something new, and they can apply it to making space for the discomfort of new ideas.

An old phrase holds: "We often learn more from failure than success." So if you offend someone by an inadvertent mistake, you have the opportunity to learn from the situation.

Let's look at the possibility of being okay with pain lighting the way to the Divine Aha! In my example about learning new ways to address an audience, I experienced a new realization as part of my Divine Aha!

"Some of my ideas may be new and uncomfortable to certain audience members. It's like switching to rap music in the middle of a Mozart concert. I've lived with these ideas.

It's important for me to slow down at times. Then I can gently offer the audience time to stir the new idea into 'their soup.' "

In a way, that one painful, intense critique did me a favor. Ever since then, I have found it valuable to slow down, sit down for some moments and quietly connect with my audiences. So some of my best learning has been in response to tough times.

Talk About What You're Learning

During interviews with people who have made their dreams come true, I discovered that they were teachable and coachable. Researchers mention that many people are most teachable after their first heart attack. But the good news is that many of us can open up to learning life's lessons with less pain and danger. When I felt shaken by that unfavorable critique, I talked with my dear friends. I took responsibility and said, "What I'm learning is …" I also contacted a personal coach to get another perspective.

Write About What You're Learning

This chapter began as notes in my personal journal. We need to make space to learn life's lessons. Your life is important. It's worth you writing about it. I often write about things that I want to cherish as my life lessons.

For example, I once heard a speaker tell about a speech he gave when he was 20 years old. In his audience, a woman said, "Young man, I'm 72 years old. Why should I listen to you?" He replied, "I heard that we teach what we need to learn. Tonight, I'm going to talk about love and forgiveness. I guess I need to learn about them." The woman replied,

"Young man, you have my attention."

This story reminds me to be genuine and let go of the idea of trying to be perfect.

Be Gentle with Yourself

The night that I was reeling from the painful comments in the particular critical review, I wrote notes while wrapped in a favorite blanket and entranced by soothing music from the motion picture soundtrack *Somewhere in Time*. These were ways of being good to myself. And I repeated the process in writing this chapter to communicate with you—from my heart to your heart.

As my clients and audiences learn communication skills, I gently share this idea:

"To communicate is like tossing Nerf balls, and some people catch them—and some do not. The idea is to get better at tossing the Nerf balls more closely and gently to others. You can do everything right, and still someone may not feel like catching the Nerf ball."

You'll feel better as you tell yourself: "I learn from everything." This is part of healthy humility. In a particular moment, we have perceptions. And good questions can help us reach the next level as we go deeper than our surface perceptions.

When you seek to heal a relationship with the offended person, you can explore these questions:
- What is my part in this situation?
- What can I learn here?
- How can I approach the person in a gentle way that he or she would prefer?
- Is it possible that I did my best and the other person was just closed off to connecting with me?

It is helpful to write in your personal journal, what you are learning—especially as the lessons come in with some pain attached.

There is no coming to consciousness without pain. - Carl Jung

Forgiveness and Your Happiness

How You Can Work Well with the Offended Person

In his book *You Can Be Happy No Matter What,* Dr. Richard Carlson wrote: "Don't attach conditions on your happiness."

This applies to you staying in a calm state of being and being able to transfer your positive energy to the offended person. In a nutshell, we're talking about using a definition of forgiveness that supports your happiness. If you're a happy person (generally), you'll have more patience and strength to keep making overtures toward the offended person.

One of Richard Carlson's main points is that we can let go of a particular thought and, perhaps, avoid related negative thoughts that can create a bad mood. He also notes that a bad mood can obscure creative solutions. Instead, it's helpful to make choices to support our well-being.

For example, I was driving with a friend who has clinical depression. Sometimes, it is a heavy load to interact with this person. My friend said with a typical energy-draining whine, "I'm tired. My feet hurt." I had the thought, "I wish that, in this relationship, I was not the only person carrying hope—and creating positive energy." Now, at that moment, I was on the edge of an emotional cliff. I could have added, "Marcus, here, doesn't do a thing to help me feel better ... "

Instead, in that moment, I chose to stop the possible

negative spiral of additional painful thoughts. I chose to focus on the positive things in that particular moment: a blue sky, and we were fortunate to have a car. I then thought about how we're fortunate to be able to see and hear. And with that, I turned on the car's radio for a possible energizing song to hear.

In just seconds, I thought of something else, which kept me in a positive mood.

I chose to not attach a condition on my happiness. My friend does not need to change so I can be happy or "proven right." I don't need to be proven right so I can be happy. I chose to let go of trying to present my case for actively seeking positive thoughts. If my friend wants to hear what I think about the subject, he can ask me—or read one of my books.

A man is rich in proportion to the number of things he can afford to let alone. - Henry David Thoreau

At this point, let's look at "rich" in terms of peace, calm and poise.

Can you imagine how much more effective you would be in building a peaceful resolution with the offended person if you were—in yourself—peaceful, calm and poised?

So I invite you to come up with a pattern to remind yourself that, in each moment, you have a choice. For example, my client Sara silently repeats this idea: "It's just a thought. Let it flow away." This is a good practice for things that are not in our control—like a loved one's current mood.

Also I have a phrase: *Catch yourself in a moment of happiness.* As I write these words, I'm in a moment of happiness.

All the happiness in the world comes from thinking of others; all the suffering in the world comes from thinking of only oneself.
- Shanti Deva

I add, Think of others, act and get caught up in the adventure. What I mean is that while you are helping someone else, you get caught up in the exhilaration of the moment.

Remember to listen to your deepest heart.

How do you listen to your heart? You ask essential questions such as:

- Who are you?
- What do you want?

Give yourself quiet time, and notice how your answers change. At this moment, I feel I am a happy spiritual being connected with Higher Power and people.

And, I want to continue my adventure expressed as: "I help people experience enthusiasm, love and wisdom to fulfill big dreams." Other desires, including supporting my loved ones, more world travel, directing motion pictures and joyful prosperity, fall under my "I help people" umbrella. That is, as I help more people, more financial abundance comes into my life.

Every year, I do things I have never done before. And in this spirit, I invite you to write in your personal journal. Identify your answers to:

- Who are you?
- What do you want?

* * *

As I have mentioned before, when you are seeking to restore a personal or business relationship, you need to nurture yourself.

During such a tough time, many people find comfort and renewal in exploring a spiritual connection. Actor Alan Arkin said, "Success is achieving what works for you inside." At one time, Alan was considered one of the top three actors in the world—but he felt great discomfort.*

* To help you make extraordinary progress, please consider my book *Nothing Can Stop You This Year!*
   http://amzn.to/SVyVK1

Since discovering meditation and a personal spiritual path, Alan said, "I find our association with the universe and God to be extremely comforting."

F. Murray Abraham won great fame and an Oscar with his role as Salieri in the motion picture Amadeus. Later, he was in a car struck by another—and, sadly, two young men died. Rescuers had to cut the actor out of his car. He went into depression, asking, "Why had I been spared?"

"To act!" his friend said. F. Murray Abraham then decided, "Acting is my gift and my obligation to God."

There are no great acts. There are small acts done with great love. - Mother Teresa

I invite you to find your gift. Also, find your comforts. (Yes, I'm listening to my favorite music as I write these words.)

Find ways to be okay with pain as it lights your path to your Divine Aha!

Many blessings on your journey.

Principle
Heal by listening to your body, your heart and your relationships.

Power Question
How can you remind yourself to listen? (Posted notes on the mirror, books on listening, etc.)

CONCLUSION OF CHAPTER TWO

We have explored the H.E.A.L. process:

H – Humor
E – Energize
A – Act
L – Listen

Remember, that the Secret Influence Process begins with you strengthening yourself. When facing tough feelings and situations, we have tools for working with illness or unease in our lives. Your Secret Charisma, which I also call Warm Trust Charisma, requires energy. When you use the H.E.A.L. process, you'll have personal energy to make warm connections with people.

We have been looking at how to heal when life's too much. We can help ourselves when we use Humor, then we Energize, Act and Listen.

When we feel life's too much, it is often that we're "too much." That is, we're too much in a hurry, or too distracted. Or we're allowing unhealthy thought patterns to run us. An old expression holds, "Some people think the same things they thought last week and last year. These people are not living ten years; they are living one year ten times."

The powerful way to heal when life's too much is to stay open and continue searching for new ways to grow and learn. Keep reading, listening to audio programs and attending workshops and spiritual gatherings.

Stop being "too much." Get out of your own way. Enlist the assistance of medical professionals, other healers, spiritual teachers, coaches, friends and family members. You can feel better.

Let's remember that in order to give to others (including the offended person) we need to keep ourselves in good shape mentally, physically and spiritually. Continually impact yourself with healing and nurturing materials.

Decision-making is easy if your values are clear.
- Roy O. Disney (Walt Disney's brother and partner)

You have the power to choose your beliefs and choose how you live on a daily basis. You can choose to focus on scarcity or abundance. You can remind yourself with "I am grateful for ... "

As I mentioned earlier, before I go to sleep each night, I write in my Daily Journal of Victories and Blessings. A victory relates to an action I took, such as exercising. A blessing is a gift, such as talking on the telephone with an extended family member. I go to sleep feeling grateful for the blessings and adventures of each day.

I am grateful for the opportunity to connect with you through this book. I wish you a journey of love, abundance and blessings.

In Chapter Three, *Say YES to Yourself: Reduce Stress and Increase Ease,* you'll learn more ways to strengthen yourself and to positively influence the offended person toward healing your personal or business relationship.

Let's continue …

CHAPTER THREE: SAY "YES" TO YOURSELF
(Reduce Stress and Increase Ease)

In Chapter One, you learned to ask gentle questions to help the offended person express his or her pain and start the healing process.

In Chapter Two, you learned to strengthen yourself and enhance your own healing.

Now, in Chapter Three, we will explore reducing stress and increasing ease. Our focus point is to *Say YES to Yourself.*

Why is this important?

Because the offended person is saying a big no to you. In essence the offended person is denying that you have any good intentions. It is as if one mistake wiped clear every kind word and every self-sacrificing effort you have ever done. If the offended person is your partner, friend or family member, this is truly painful.

This whole section on the Secret Influence Process is vital to your being at your best so you radiate Your Secret Charisma. The person who get to a calm state of being can improve relationships, both personal and business. That's the essence of Warm Trust Charisma.

As I mentioned earlier, the Secret Influence Process includes:

- Strengthen yourself
- Remain in a calm state of being
- Communicate your concern and kindness
- Take action with the F.A.R. methods (forgiveness, amends, regret)

When I give my presentation *Say YES to Yourself: Reduce Stress and Increase Ease* in a hospital or association meeting, I notice that the attendees welcome the opportunity to learn how to enhance their personal energy.

Imagine that you want to have the energy to:

- Shine at work and look good to your boss
- Persuade customers
- Be good to your loved ones when you return from a workday
- Withstand the emotional storms of the offended person

Wouldn't it be great to be able to flow with any change that comes up in the office? To stand strong and not be knocked flat. Instead, you can have the skills to respond to any stressful situation effectively; to have calm and poise; to demonstrate effective leadership. And, let's face it, to just feel better as you go through your day. That's what we're going to discuss here in Chapter Three.

We will explore the S.A.Y.Y.E.S. process:

S – Step off the stage
A – Accept better care
Y – Yield to recovery

Y – Yearn for energy
E – Encourage your best
S – Support your team

When you learn these methods, you will also expand your feelings of confidence.

Let's stride forward to better days ...

STEP OFF THE STAGE
(#1 of the S.A.Y.Y.E.S. Process)

Do you frequently feel that you have to be on your guard when in front of other people? How much time do you get for relaxing?

By "stage" I mean anywhere you're with people. Being on stage is anytime when you feel some amount of social pressure. The point is that you need to recharge as you go through your day.

Let's remember that the Secret Influence Process requires that you guard your energy so that you can patiently listen to the offended person.

We don't stop playing because we grow old; we grow old because we stop playing. - George Bernard Shaw

The person who steps off the stage simply feels better. Part of feeling better is to have some time for relaxation and, yes, playing.

Researchers note that the most effective people use this pattern: activity then recovery.

What does this look like? It can be as simple as one hour working on a report—that's the Activity part. Then, you get up, step outside your office and walk around the block. That's the Recovery part.

Then back to work. My clients often find that a five minute walk—their form of recovery—energizes them to return to activities that require concentration.

People need to become what's known as a corporate athlete. A corporate athlete is an expert on using energy and replenishing energy. Corporate athletes pay attention, and learn their personal style of using energy and replenishing energy. And they make effective plans to use the Activity-Recovery pattern.

It takes a lot of energy to keep up your professional face. It's a façade. You need times during your workday when you can catch your breath, and step away from other people. This is what I mean by "step off the stage."

Just a little time will do. Years ago, I worked for a particular organization in downtown San Francisco. There was no spare room at this firm. During my lunch break, I would step on to the balcony with a chair, sit down and meditate. You can rest in a restroom stall—if necessary. You can go to your car and rest there. You can rest by walking on the steps between floors. Here is a question to ask yourself:

Power Question: How can I step off the stage?

A Power Question is a trigger. Top professionals use positive triggers to shift how they respond to things that come up during their workday. Each of us can use a Power Question to get us thinking of better actions.

The easiest way to see this distinction is to think of the opposite. Here's an Energy-Draining Question: "Why does this always happen to me?" Ow. I can feel it. I'm leaking energy! Help!

Now let's look at the opposite, two Power Questions: "How can I turn this around? Who can help me?"

That's it! Now, I feel like myself! Strong, poised, confident. I feel that I have resources.

Awareness and action

In many years of coaching clients, guiding audiences and speaking to students at Stanford University and Academy of Art University, I learned that to increase success and fulfillment, we need two things: awareness and action.

When I share with you a S.A.Y.Y.E.S. method, we're increasing awareness. When we use the Power Question, we're using a positive trigger to get you going with effective action.

If you normally maintain a packed schedule, take five minutes between appointments to return a call to a friend. Laugh a little. Take your mind off things.

At other times, get away from others and give yourself the gift of silence. Take a brief walk. Sit in your car and listen to soothing music.

Music washes away from the soul the dust of everyday life.
- Berthold Auerbach

Each one of these brief actions is a way to step off the stage. Like a brief, mini-vacation, it is your moment to get away from other people and energize yourself.

This mini-vacation is crucial. Why? Because part of the F.A.R. process is sincerely expressing regret. And it is tough to remain in the painful, regretful place.

So be sure to get some time away from the offended person so you can recharge your batteries. The truth is the offended person wants you to express regret and to feel sad and in pain.

A human being often needs a break! So get time away, and get off the stage.

Principle
Step off the stage (give yourself recovery time).

Power Question
How can you step off the stage? (Write a list of five things you can do at different points in your day.)

ACCEPT BETTER CARE
(#2 of the S.A.Y.Y.E.S. Process)

Imagine seeing your best friend working in the manner you do. Would you counsel him or her to take an appropriate break? It is likely that you would. Here is the important question to ask yourself repeatedly through the workday:

How can I take better care of myself right now?

Progress is impossible without change, and those who cannot change their minds cannot change anything.
- George Bernard Shaw

We need nutrition, exercise, sleep and health care. Treating ourselves as worthwhile [people] helps us feel worthwhile. [Give your] soul a better home. - Touchstones, A Book of Daily Meditations for Men

To accept better care is a powerful process for healing. Many of us get so caught up in our work that we do not take care of ourselves.

Many people find comfort through spiritual practices. Here is a prayer that enriches many lives.

The Serenity Prayer
God grant me the serenity to accept the things I cannot change, courage to change the things I can, and wisdom to know the difference. - Reinhold Niebuhr

Pull out your personal journal and write down the Power

Question: *How can I take better care of myself right now?*
Then quickly, in 20 seconds, write down six ways you can take action to nurture yourself.

There is more to life than increasing its speed.
- Mahatma Gandhi

Your healthy functioning is where your wisdom lies, it is your peace of mind, your common sense, your satisfaction in life, and your feeling of wholeness. - Richard Carlson

In other words, healthy functioning consists of the moments when you have felt good! Some of us are going through tough times and we may find it hard to remember when we felt good. Okay. Recall a moment of laughter. For example, when my sweetheart came through an operation that removed her spleen, she said, "Well, I'm lighter now." That was a moment of humor.

Healthy functioning is when a human being is living in the moment and in an authentic way. On the other hand, each of us has a thought system. This is a pattern of thinking that was set up in childhood. If your parents argued about money, then some part of you thinks, "Money is a source of arguments." That is not a solid, stuck-in-the-cement truth. Talk to enough people and you will hear different ideas, such as, "Money is a source for planning." Or my comment:

Money is a tool I use well for the benefit of all. - Tom Marcoux

"You can't satisfy your thought system," wrote Richard Carlson. The point is that when you fall back into your thought system, you are likely to get stuck in other dark or sad thoughts.

It's impossible to feel gratitude for something when you are too busy trying to improve it. - Richard Carlson

Imagine, taking a breath and enjoying the moment of sitting with a family member. Imagine just being grateful that you're both still here, on this planet. "Gratitude is the antidote to depression," Richard Carlson declared.

Light is more powerful than darkness. Healthy functioning is more powerful than unhappiness ... You don't find light by studying the dark. - Richard Carlson

From this statement, we can realize that a balance is needed. Certainly, it sometimes helps to reflect on what may be an unhealthy pattern of behavior in your life. At one point, I noticed that I had chosen a series of partners who were emotionally shut down. At that point, I ended the unhealthy relationship I was in.

So an insight can give you some energy to take a new step forward.

On the other hand, studying every bad mistake and bad feeling can become overdone. As mentioned earlier, Richard wrote, You don't find light by studying the dark.

So let's balance things out by focusing on the light! This is a source of healing. What is light and wholesome in your life? Well, you can read! Or someone is reading this to you.

So let's take that step in healing: reach toward the light.

How do we do this? We make a choice in the moment.

For example, my client Stephen had an argument with his father on the phone one evening. It had been a 12-hour workday for Stephen, a CEO. He mentioned that he made a thousand decisions that day. His father, a retired blue-collar worker, scoffed at that idea. Like a knee-jerk reaction,

Stephen felt angry. His tone of voice was intense, and he ended the conversation abruptly.

After the phone call, at midnight, Stephen recalled the conversation and felt remorse.

Stephen had a choice; one option was to obsess over his errors in the conversation. And if he continued on that path, Stephen could recall every irritable conversation he had ever had with his father. Or Stephen could choose the second option: to let the negative thought flow away—as if on a river.

It helped that Stephen chose to write briefly about the situation in his personal journal. He wrote:

"Next time, I'll remind myself that my happiness does not depend on being proven right. It doesn't depend on my father understanding my situation. He can't really. He's lived with a separate psychological reality. His blue-collar work was different than my corporate work."

Then, Stephen let his negative thoughts drift away. To help with this, he reached for his iPod and listened to some soothing music.

And in making this decision and choosing to let go of negative thoughts, Stephen was giving himself better care.

Let's remember that if you take care of yourself well, you will have more energy to devote to restoring your relationship with the offended person.

Principle
Focus on accepting better care.

Power Question
How can I take better care of myself right now?

YIELD TO RECOVERY
(#3 of the S.A.Y.Y.E.S. Process)

When do you appropriately yield in your life?

When we drive a car, we must often yield to oncoming traffic. And in life, we must yield to the truth that researchers discovered about optimal human functioning: humans do best when they use an Activity-Recovery Pattern. This means that the person is active and then rests for an appropriate period of time. Top tennis pros, in a two-hour match, are active for 20 minutes. They rest in between outbursts of energy. For an office worker, the person can write a report in the morning, then later "rest" by doing something less taxing—perhaps, some photocopying.

Taking responsibility to get away [for a break]is a good cure for self-pity and exhaustion.
- Touchstones, A Book of Daily Meditations for Men

Here is a helpful question: *How can I use the Activity-Recovery Pattern?*

The Calm-Tai Chi Movement

Special breathing and movement release tension from the body. During my presentations, the audience enjoys The Calm-Tai Chi Movement, which comes from the combination of my degree in psychology and training in Asian movement.

Stand with your feet apart as wide as your shoulders.

Bend your knees slightly. Now, raise your arms in front of you, palms down and open. Once your arms are stretched out in front of you with your hands at shoulder height, gently pull your hands back toward your shoulders.

Then gently lower your hands until your hands are loosely hanging at your thigh level.

A number of Tai Chi DVDs are available in stores and online—so that you can see what I have just described.

My addition is for you to add what I call Affirm-Breathing. As you breathe in say an affirmation silently in your mind, such as: I am relaxing, or God relaxes me, or Higher Power holds me safe.

As your lower your hands, breathe out and again silently say your affirmation.

Quiet time (prayer, meditation, more)

A major proponent of meditation was asked, "How long do you meditate each day?"

"Three minutes," the spiritual teacher replied. He emphasized that a consistent three-minute daily habit was more beneficial than an unfulfilled intention to do a 20-minute meditation daily session.

Do three minutes help? Ask my sweetheart. She has seen how I become much more at ease when I take even a mere three minutes on a train to devote to quiet time and deep breathing.

Carry a timer in your briefcase or purse and discover the benefit of at least three minutes of quiet time. Please realize that connection with Higher Power can happen in an instant. So three minutes truly can bring you tangible peace.

Principle
Be sure to yield to recovery time.

Power Question
How can you use the Activity-Recovery Pattern?

YEARN FOR ENERGY
(#4 of the S.A.Y.Y.E.S. Process)

One day in my office, I felt so drained that I could barely sit up in my chair. My usual lively energy had vanished and I was afraid. This moment reminded me of a time when I was in a cave. The cave guide had us turn off all lights. Complete darkness. I could not see my hand, which was only three inches in front of my eyes. For a second, I felt almost a weight of darkness.

What can you do if you feel a heavy burden at work? The human mind has a terrific "switch" built in. Just like in a cave, you do not fight darkness with darkness. You light one candle. For the human mind, the candle is a question.

A prudent question is one-half of wisdom. - Francis Bacon

That tough day when I had significant work to do, I was feeling cast adrift and with no connection. In a quiet place in my rational mind, I knew that this report would somehow ultimately serve a number of people. But I needed that "switch." So I asked myself, "Where is the joy?"

Then I realized the joy was a few steps out in the future. My joy would occur when I would speak before an audience (using the ideas of the report). The fun would be sharing the ideas and creating humor in the moment.

That was where the joy was. At that point, I had a connection to the purpose for the report, and I felt energetic.

Power Question: Where is the joy?

Gain Energy through Talk, Walk, Write

You can call a friend (or even speak into an audio recording device) and gain energy. Just talk about the project and then ask aloud, "Where is the joy?"

Then your mind starts looking for the answer. You could say, "Where is the joy? I don't know. I guess the joy is ... " And your mind will ultimately fill in the blank. It helps to write down your answer, so later, you can review and support your energy.

Often we feel sluggish because our body actually craves to move. So how about combine "talk" and "walk." Take a walk and use your cell phone (or audio recording device).

Energy, Money, and Healing

Many of us lose so much energy to our habitual thoughts about money. We need to be careful about the jokes we share with friends, like, "There is more month at the end of the money."

Feeling upset does not help in our purpose of healing ourselves.

Money is a tool I use well for the benefit of all. - Tom Marcoux

Money is such a crucial topic related to healing both ourselves and our relationships that I wrote a book *10 Seconds to Wealth: Master the Moment Using Your Divine Gifts.*

Here I want to emphasize: from our thoughts come feelings. So if you have a reflexive, negative thought about money, you can switch the direction of your thoughts. Just momentarily visualize a "cancel button." Then do the motion of pressing the button and say the word "Cancel!"

Then immediately state silently an empowering replacement-thought. For example, you can remember:

Who is rich? He that rejoices in his portion.
- Benjamin Franklin

Imagine this. You are prosperous in this moment. How? It is likely that you ate breakfast. You can read this. And at this very moment, you are not on the phone arguing with a creditor. So in this moment, you are okay!

My client Serena responded to this idea with a big smile. "You're right! I am okay."

Anytime you want to feel an increase in energy, remind yourself to say: "I am grateful for _____" And fill in the blank.

The key to momentum is always having something to look forward to. - Wynn Davis

And this reminds me of the old phrase: "Happiness is something to do, someone to love and something to look forward to." Concentrate on these elements, and your energy will increase.

Remember to ask, "Where is the joy?"

Principle
Find the joy as part of what you're doing.

Power Question
Where is the joy?

Tom Marcoux

ENCOURAGE YOUR BEST
(#5 of the S.A.Y.Y.E.S. Process)

What secret do many people miss at their workplace? As you walk into stores and restaurants, how often do you see listless people who look like they're just doing time—as if in a prison?

The secret they are missing is when you do your best, you feel good. You even find fun on many occasions.

Make not your thoughts your prisons. - William Shakespeare

The thought, "Ugh! I have to do this!" drains energy like holes in a water tower.

When I first began working at the age of 15, I found myself one summer working five days a week at Levi Strauss, weekends for A & W Restaurant and one evening a week for Underwriter's Laboratory. One thing that sustained me was having these thoughts:

Wherever I am, I will serve. And I'll make friends.
- Tom Marcoux

I realized that whatever job I was doing, I had the opportunity to do my best and feel good about the whole thing.

Just do what must be done. This may not be happiness, but it is greatness. - George Bernard Shaw

No one ever got excited about doing barely enough to get by. And many people hold great fear about their jobs. The solution is to become known for being excellent in the skills highly valued in your particular workplace. Ask yourself, "What am I best known for?" Then, make sure that you do what will help you be known as a crucial team member.

The question "What am I best known for?" is a pillar of your personal brand. A personal brand does for an individual what a product brand does for a company. In essence, the personal brand is a clear and brief message of what you offer and what the listener can trust you to do.

In my book *Nothing Can Stop You This Year*, I relate a number of personal branding strategies. And, here let's focus on how helpful it is for you to hone your message about your work into these two areas:

- "This is what I offer."
- "You can trust me to listen carefully to your concerns, devise an appropriate process, and come through for you."

Top performers repeatedly talk about how they honed their skills with their natural talents. They express their natural brilliance. Researchers are now emphasizing that success goes to those people who choose to accentuate their strengths and delegate to others who have better skills or inherent talent in other areas.

In your personal journal, answer these questions:

- What are my strengths?
- How can I express my strengths vividly so people know what I offer is exceptional?
- How can I get help in areas that do not coincide with my strengths?

For example, I rely on a team of people who demonstrate talent in editing, accounting, illustrating, filming and more. This has set me free to continually hone my talents in speaking, writing, directing films, leading various teams and guiding people to communicate powerfully.

Focus on your strengths and express your natural brilliance.

Principle
Focus on expressing your personal brilliance.

Power Question
What are you best known for?

SUPPORT YOUR TEAM
(#6 of the S.A.Y.Y.E.S. Process)

Describe a team. What do the team members share? A feeling of connection. Often, a common dedication to one goal. At Pepsi, they had one goal, which they verbalized in two words: "Beat Coke."

Secret influence truly occurs when you look on the other person as part of your team. You work with him or her. You communicate in ways that make it easy for the person to take in your message.

*Do **not** do unto others as you expect they should do unto you. Their tastes may not be the same. - George Bernard Shaw*

In order to experience support from your co-workers and supervisor, you need to first support them. This starts the flow of good will. They are all true individuals with different personality styles. In my book *Darkest Secrets of Persuasion and Seduction Masters: Protect Yourself and Turn the Power to Good*, I present a number of facets of personality styles. Here, we'll cover a brief overview. Personality styles can be described in this manner:

The Lion: A director-type person who is a hard-charger with little patience. This person wants to hear the brief details and to know the impact on the bottom line.

The Dog: A relater-type person who values a human connection over changing to make things better. This person likes routine.

The Beaver: An analytic-type person who is a detail

obsessed, engineer-type person. Often, this person is slow to make a decision.

The Peacock: A socializer-type person who loves talking about ideas with people, and who is quick at decision making and often poor on follow-up.

Here's an example. My client Theresa was presenting to a group of people and she took into account their personality styles.

* * *

Personality Style
Theresa's Methods

Beaver ("analytic" or "engineer" or "accountant")

Theresa used a list of methods that she formed into a process: P.R.E.S.E.N.T.

Dog ("relater")

Theresa asked audience members, "What are you hoping or expecting that I will be talking about today?" Then, she wrote down their topics and questions.

Lion ("director")

Theresa checked off the topics/questions as she went through them. The director-type person appreciates seeing progress shown by checking off the topics.

Peacock ("socializer")

Prior to her talk, Theresa walked around the room and met the audience members. She wrote down people's comments. She shared some comments in this manner: "I was talking with Tony, and he mentioned that the XYZ works best when … How about a round of applause for Tony?"

* * *

Here is another example. John has a "director" (Lion) style, and he compensates for it. In the middle of a conversation with Susan, a relater (Dog), John slows down and asks gentle questions. He listens first.

Know your tendencies and compensate for them.
- Tom Marcoux

John takes a different but helpful approach when working with Matt, an analyzer (Beaver), John invites Matt to prepare in a special way before their next weekly meeting. John says, "Matt, write some notes on three alternative solutions. Then endorse one and tell me your reasoning when we meet on Friday." In this manner, John supports Matt's analytic personality style. John also supports his own "director" personality style that calls for brevity.

Learn about the personality styles and tailor your message to the individual. Also, realize that the offended person is likely the opposite from you in personality traits. So tread softly. Communicate in a way that the offended person can easily take in your message.

Principle

Learn to flow and support personality styles—to enhance joy and harmony in relationships.

Power Question

How can personality styles help you do better?

CONCLUSION TO CHAPTER THREE

In Chapter Three, we have covered the S.A.Y.Y.E.S. process:

S – Step off the stage
A – Accept better care
Y – Yield to recovery
Y – Yearn for energy
E – Encourage your best
S – Support your team

Remember, the essence of secret influence is to nurture yourself, place yourself in a calm state of being and then encourage the transfer of your calm state of being to the offended person.

In *Chapter Four, Effectively Work with Creditors so You Can Get Out of Debt and Back on Your Feet*, we will explore how you can bring more peace to your daily life. From that foundation, you can have more energy to devote to healing your relationship with the offended person.

Let's move forward …

CHAPTER FOUR: WORK EFFECTIVELY WITH CREDITORS
(Get out of Debt and Back on Your Feet)

What causes major breakups of romantic couples? Money troubles. What creates anxiety for many people? Intimidating calls from creditors and collection agencies.

If you are upset in relation to money troubles, it is hard to have the energy to remain patient when dealing with the offended person.*

---

* At the time of this writing, people are dealing with doctor/hospital bills, disabilities, long-term unemployment, family member addiction, and legal fees. Top financial advisors, including Suze Orman, suggest contacting resources including the National Foundation for Credit Counseling (nfcc.org). Some people find it necessary to seek local resources like a food bank or a shelter or sign up for reduced utility bills when income is low. Suze Orman discusses the true last resort of bankruptcy, and she recommends the overview at www.credit.com/slp/chapter8/Bankruptcy.jsp. On the Fair Debt Collection Practices Act (FDCPA), which limits the actions creditors can take, she recommends the discussion at
 www.credit.com/credit_information/credit_law/Understanding-Your-Debt-Collection-Rights.jsp#2

So this section will help you improve tough situations. I first shared this information in my book *Truth No One Will Tell You.*

When I looked up "debt quotes" with Google.com, I noticed an interesting label: "Debt quotes/Financial Responsibility."

Empower yourself by seeing responsibility as the ability to respond. In this section, we will arm you with methods so that you can respond. You'll learn how to talk with creditors in ways to set up reasonable repayment schedules.

As I mentioned earlier, the Secret Influence Process includes:

1. Strengthen yourself
2. Remain in a calm state of being
3. Communicate your concern and kindness
4. Take action with the F.A.R. methods (forgiveness, amends, regret)

Remember, when you nurture yourself you can go into a calm state of being. Secret influence occurs when you transfer that calm state of being to the offended person. At that point, eventually, the offended person will drop his or her blinders and, perhaps, recall your past kind and helpful actions.

An interviewer asked me, "How do you transfer positive energy to the offended person?"

I replied: "Through your eyes, body movements, smile and vocal tonality. We communicate constantly. The offended person picks up all the subtle cues. If you have positive energy inside, it naturally radiates out from you."

Sometimes a profound idea appears very simple:

If you want to be rich, solve problems. - Robert Kiyosaki

If you solve important problems at work, you are likely to gain raises and promotions.

If you create a product and it solves problems, you are likely to gain a significant number of customers.

In fact, I was inspired to write this section because I recalled the idea solve problems. This led me to the question: What problem dominates people's thoughts? Money troubles. To be at your best and to radiate Your Secret Charisma, you need to take action so you avoid being distracted by money troubles.

When it comes to debt, the target is to learn how to turn things around. We will use the T.U.R.N. process:

T – Talk
U – Understand
R – Right-size
N – Nurture

Let's step forward …

TALK
(#1 of the T.U.R.N. Process)

What's one of the most important things a person needs to do if he or she can't pay their bills?

Talk to the creditors. You heard that right.

You must call credit card collectors, tell them the truth and deal with your situation head-on. - Suze Orman

In this section we will cover:
• How to ask for lower payments
• How to create a positive atmosphere during the call so that the person is more likely to cooperate
• How to ask to talk with a supervisor and how to flow with the conversation once the supervisor arrives

The Benefit of Making Arrangements with Creditors

Once you make arrangements to make small payments toward your debts, you'll feel better in some important ways.

Keeping what you have and creating what you deserve is not only about money. It is about the absence of fear, which is an even greater blessing than the absence of want; and fear tends to disappear when you tell the truth. - Suze Orman

How to Ask for Lower Payments

First, rehearse with a friend so that you feel you're ready. Also have your notes in front of you. The clerk on the phone will not see that you have your notes and a "script" in front of you.

Courage is easier when I'm prepared. - Tom Marcoux

Second, before you dial the phone number be sure to sit down and make sure you have calmed down. My client Marina found that she felt better after she chose an affirmation and repeated it before calling a creditor. Her choice was: "God holds me safe." An affirmation can work when it is personal and means something to your heart.

Once you dial and have a creditor's team member on the line, you can say something like: "Hello, I want to set up a payment arrangement ... "

Please know that even a small payment of even $5.00 is a demonstration of good faith. It is truly a good start. At this point, the person on the other side is feeling good—at least a little bit. The creditor has someone calling her and seeking to make the situation better. Good for you!

An interviewer asked, "Won't some creditors say, 'That's not enough,' and then say something intimidating and require at least $50.00?"

Yes. That can happen. However, if you start making payments, you'll see that creditors will usually cash the checks. Also, you are creating a good history of taking positive action.

You can say, "I can only send $5.00 at this time. I'm certainly looking to make this better. And I am aiming to make a good start now."

How to create a positive atmosphere during the call so that the person is more likely to cooperate

The idea is to turn the creditor into a friendly associate. You do this by expressing appreciation.

If properly appreciated, we feel better ... We become more open to listening and more motivated to cooperate ... You are more likely to reach a wise agreement than if each side feels unappreciated. - Roger Fisher and Daniel Shapiro

So as soon as possible in your conversation with the creditor, say sincerely, "I appreciate how you're making this as pleasant as possible."

As a side note, years ago, I found that I often gained cooperation quickly (even when getting a vendor to correct his mistake) by starting my conversation with: "I'm hoping you'll have good news for me."

How to communicate with the supervisor

Sometimes the first person you talk with truly cannot help you. They are likely bound by policies that hold no flexibility. The person often starts merely repeating himself, and says that he cannot do what you're asking for. But the supervisor often has more leeway.

You can say, "Well, it looks like it's time to talk with your supervisor."

Sometimes, you need to maintain a firm voice and keep repeating your request. You may need to ask, "Are you saying I cannot talk with the supervisor?" Your conversation is being recorded, and it is likely that the clerk on the phone does not want to be caught telling something that is not true. So he may pass you to the supervisor at that point.

There are times when you need to say, "Oh, something is happening here. I'm going to have to hang up now." And then you end the call. The reason for this strategy is that when you call back, you may be fortunate to get a different clerk. In any case, be prepared to repeatedly, firmly and politely ask to speak with a supervisor. (I have found it helpful to even call another time and get a different supervisor.)

When you talk with the supervisor, gently ask for his or her name with: "Hello, I'm [your name]. And you are … ?"

A few times during the conversation add appreciative comments while using the person's name. You can say, "Trina, I appreciate your helping me with this." You may need to ask the supervisor to repeat an explanation or detail, and you can say, "Oh. I appreciate you giving me that information. Would you please repeat the part about XYZ, I'm putting that into my notes."

When you say the above you are expressing appreciation and you are giving a quiet alert that you are taking notes.

* * *

A place for truth-telling … with your friends and your family

A number of people get into significant credit card debt by charging vacations and consumer goods. To get out of debt, it will be necessary to change habits.

One time, my sweetheart and I wanted to take a vacation with friends. But then a project did not yield the funds that we had expected. So I had to call our friends and tell the truth: my sweetheart and I could not attend because a project had not worked out as planned. Over the years, I have made it a practice to save up in advance before taking a vacation.

In fact, I know a couple who saved for five years so that they could go on a cruise.

Never spend your money before you have it. - Thomas Jefferson

Good Debt versus Bad Debt

It is true that there are some expenses that are valuable enough for using "good debt." For many people, getting a college education leads to a higher paying, more satisfying job—so student loans would be "good debt." But going into debt to buy the latest consumer goods, such as a top-flight home entertainment system, may not be a match for building a life with financial abundance.

Good debt could be an appropriate business loan. For example, one time I gained a loan for a project that later gave me credibility. This credibility led to my later gaining $223,760. To me that was good debt. Basically, the answer is this: "Good debt involves creating a true asset." A college education can be a true asset. My business project was a true asset. You get the picture.

As this is being written, many Americans have been hit by a foreclosure crisis in that they had agreed to variable rates related to their mortgages. So it essential that you get legal advice to make sure that a loan agreement will not have clauses that could result in harm for you. Be sure to get advice from someone who is on your side—that is, a person who does not have an agenda in conflict with your well-being. (For example, be aware that various mortgage vendors truly want to close the deal with you; that's how the vendors get paid.)

Make informed choices and you can improve your financial situation.

Principle
Rehearse before you talk to creditors.

Power Question
Which friends or family members can help you through good rehearsals before you talk to creditors?

UNDERSTAND
(#2 of the T.U.R.N. Process)

Understand this: if the creditor gets any kind of payment from you, the creditor feels as if he or she is winning. Making a $5.00 payment is a good start. Financial advisors such as David Bach and Suze Orman emphasize that it is often advisable to pay the highest interest loan or credit card first.

In this section, we're talking about secret influence to get you out of trouble, and here I want to emphasize that you can influence a creditor to improve a situation. For example, financial advisors note that you can search out the lowest interest rate credit cards, and armed with this information you can return to your own credit card vendor and encourage them to lower your rate. The credit card vendor would rather retain you as customer than to lose you to another credit card company. It is important for you to study reputable sources of financial information so that you have the tools and information you need to improve your situation.

If you feed your mind as often as you feed your stomach, then you'll never have to worry about feeding your stomach or a roof over your head or clothes on your back. - Albert Einstein

Often, we notice that many people who truly succeed had to work two jobs simultaneously—for years. For example, Albert Einstein worked as a clerk in a patent office while he pondered light, space and time. In 1905, while working in that patent office, Einstein had four papers published in the

Annalen der Physik, the leading German physics journal. Physicists to this day look on these papers as significant achievements. And Albert Einstein did two things simultaneously: he worked to make a living and he pursued the area of his natural brilliance to make a life.

Principle
Understand that you'll need to do extraordinary things: study financial information and perhaps, work more than one job.

Power Questions
Where do your talents and skills actually reside? Could you invest in yourself by taking a class or getting coaching to help you turn a hobby into a side source of income? (Today's economy often requires people to develop multiple sources of income.)

RIGHT-SIZE
(#3 of the T.U.R.N. Process)

What do many chronic debtors have in common? Their lives are out of balance; in other words, their lives are "wrong-sized." For our discussion, a definition of wrong-sized includes these elements noted by experts who assist people to recover from financial mistakes.

"Wrong-sized" means:
- A person's expenditures have exceeded his or her income

- A person uses the act of buying stuff to feel some pleasure and to numb some hidden pain
- The person is out of balance and uses stuff to distract him or her from her pain or sense of emptiness

If you borrow $10,000 on your credit cards and pay only the minimum payment with an interest rate of $19.98%, it will take you more than 37 years to get out of debt ... [and] you will have forked over nearly $19,000 in interest charges. - David Bach

Early in my working life, I learned two things. Have two nice pairs of pants and avoid using a clothes dryer on your dress shirts. By not using a dryer on my dress shirts I avoided shrinkage of my shirts—and I avoided having to buy new shirts! At that time in my life, that was an example of taking action to "right-size" my life and purchases.

Reduce the amount of your purchases. Put in safety measures so that you do not overspend. Financial advisors talk about: a) only bringing cash to the grocery store; b) batching (grouping) your errands so that you save gas money; and c) writing down a spending plan. A number of people avoid the word "budget." Instead, they use the name "spending plan" as something that can empower you to make effective choices. My clients often use the title: Financial Abundance Plan.

Remember to include some enjoyable experiences. Otherwise, you may find an unhealthy pattern occurring. For example, someone who does not eat breakfast may find herself eating a huge dinner. Deprivation can cause binge behavior. This is the reason that I am emphasizing putting a plan in place so that you have some enjoyment (on a modest scale) each month.

To set a plan and follow through does take effort.

I will do what others will not do, so in the future I can do what others cannot do. - Randy Gage

Success is having good relationships, fulfilling employment, and being as healthy as you can be. - Larry Winget

Our definition of success and our beliefs about "the good life" impact our daily actions. If a person says, "I deserve this," every time he is near the display of DVDs in a store, it is likely that he will purchase another DVD (that will eventually sit on a shelf, gathering dust).

Let's go back to Larry Winget's definition of success: Success is having good relationships, fulfilling employment, and being as healthy as you can be.

We notice that this list does not include: a car as good or better than the Jones; the best-looking house in the neighborhood; 27 pairs of shoes ...

Oh-oh! Perhaps, I have gone too far. It's true that many of us tend to have a soft spot for something (like shoes). I admit it: my soft spot is books. Early in my work life, I was strategic in how I gained books. A debuting hardcover book is most expensive. If I would demonstrate patience, I could wait for the paperback book to appear one year later. Less cost. And today, you can purchase the paperback book as a serviceable used book through Amazon.com.

An interviewer asked, "So how do we avoid making impulse purchases?"

I replied, "It's a multi-layered process. You need a plan and then to work your plan."

To Avoid Impulse Purchases and Handle Your "Soft Spot"

- Carefully choose your definition of success.
- Have safety measures; for example, go shopping with a friend who tends to save money and is careful with purchases.
- Replace troublesome behavior with helpful behavior; for example, take a walk in a park instead of a shopping mall.
- Use a Self-Nurture Chart and make sure that you experience enjoyment (without spending money) on a daily basis.

My client Kevin came to me about concerns that he might make some spending mistakes while his wife was away visiting family. Kevin wisely understood that with his wife temporarily absent, he would be experiencing loneliness and some pain. From our conversation, Kevin created his own Self-Nurture Chart.

First, Kevin identified "Nurturing Actions":
1) Reading in hot bath
2) Hot bath listening to music and resting my eyes
3) Comment in journal to Becky (wife)
4) Prayer for Becky to be safe and have a good trip
5) Tai chi (outside?)
6) Yoga (outside?)
7) Three minutes of silence
8) Have a list of friends--and call one
9) Watch episode of a funny TV show
10) Ride bicycle outside
11) Walk outside, even for 10 minutes

Second, Kevin writes "Monday through Sunday" on a grid

so he can check of how many of the 11 Nurturing Actions he accomplishes on a given day.

Kevin did at least two of these actions on each day and found that he felt better and he avoided impulse-spending.

It's all about making choices that empower you.

You may decide to increase your value to the company where you work. Or you may decide to start a company of your own on the side. Author Michael Masterson writes:

"Every successful start-up business is one that has quickly and correctly answered [these] questions: 1) What is the most cost-effective way of attracting customers? And 2) What is the best way to keep those customers buying?"

Michael Masterson emphasizes that each business needs to focus on "1) Lowering the cost of acquiring new customers and 2) Increasing the lifetime value of each existing customer."

Rather go to bed supperless than rise in debt.
- Benjamin Franklin

Now that is an extreme idea. How about we change the idea to something like: go without some lattés and fancy restaurant dinners. I have a bachelor friend who spends (not invests) thousands of dollars on eating out. Then, at one point he came across the idea: "$1,200 saved with compound interest of 8% would yield $12,000 in 30 years." At that point, he realized that he wasn't only losing $1,200 in that year, he was also losing $12,000, too!

And yet, I remember my own bachelor days in which I lived for a time on spinach, brown rice, some vegetables and tuna fish. I was saving my funds for my projects. That is, I was devoting money to building assets: projects that would gain me professional credibility.

We're talking about right-sizing your life and your expenses. And this is really about focusing on your true values and priorities.

Low overhead equals freedom. - Teller (of the team Penn and Teller)

Principle
"Right-size" your life and purchases so that you can build a future of financial abundance.

Power Questions
What is your soft spot? (Shoes? DVDs? Books?) How can you make a spending budget so that you can occasionally reward yourself with your "soft spot," but have ways to restrain yourself from going overboard?

NURTURE
(#4 of the T.U.R.N. Process)

Getting out of debt is hard work. You absolutely need to nurture yourself. You must keep your strength up.

But the big question is: what are you working for as you stretch yourself to get out of debt? *What is your big benefit?*

Financial Independence is [when] you have the resources to live a satisfying, comfortable life, accomplish your dreams and goals, and have more fun doing what you do. - Barbara Stanny

Here is a secret: You can feel financial independence now. How? This quote gives us a good direction:

We do not remember days, we remember moments.
- Cesare Pavese

The idea is to focus on times when you felt good and had what you needed to enjoy the moment. Earlier, I shared this example, and it bears repeating here. Years ago I was in Disneyland with a friend. At the time, I did not have much money. But as I looked around the theme park I felt rich—as if the whole park was there for me. Certainly, Disneyland was there for the thousands of people present in the park. But I could stroll through the theme park with a big, joyful smile on my face.

On the other hand, my friend, who also was on a limited budget, had a completely different mindset. She was upset because she could not buy everything that she had a passing fancy for in the stores. She did not enjoy the abundance of just being in Disneyland!

My point is when I looked around Disneyland and smiled, I was, in that moment, feeling financial independence. I wasn't thinking about payments to the dentist, health insurance or anything else. I was in the moment. Again, let's remember the above quote: *"We do not remember days, we remember moments."*

* * *

It is crucial that we nurture ourselves. This is especially true for those of us who have entrepreneurial pursuits. For example, there was a time I was feeling overwhelmed. I mentioned to my sweetheart, "I feel like a racehorse." She replied, *"Run in better races."*

What would "better races" be? I decided to pull back from certain activities that were not yielding the best results in both serving people and bringing in financial abundance. For example, there was a time that I chose to stop leading acting workshops. I found that my location was home to wannabe actors who had no money. So the workshops were not a lucrative way to gain income. Instead, I started to speak to people in corporate settings.

A second insight arose from the "run in better races" conversation. I thought, "If I was a racehorse, I did not want to be a stableperson, too." What that meant was that I needed to work smart and focus on doing what I was uniquely capable of doing. So I started to hire interns and contractors to work by the hour. I made a promise to myself that I would write my books but not typeset them.

We notice a difficulty for a number of people who run their own business: they burn out because they're wearing too many hats. It is better to hire independent contractors to relieve you of the burdens of bookkeeping and other tasks.

Business owners with a small budget can engage interns. For example, one of my friends recently went to a high school computer club and engaged an exceptional high school student to work on Web site-related projects.

The truth is that business owners truly need to focus on caring for current customers and gaining new customers. Once a business owner begins to work on the business instead of just in the business—the business starts to run better.

If you're a business owner and you feel overwhelmed, here is an important question: Where can you get the energy to patiently work toward healing your relationship with the offended person? Without working smart, you may be running a deficit in energy.

Pull out your personal journal and note how you might get help. Or at least how you can nurture yourself by scheduling in breaks.

The central idea about nurturing yourself

As I mentioned, getting out of debt is hard work, and you need to nurture yourself.

Here is what is important: *Find ways that do not cost money to soothe yourself, comfort yourself and put salve on your wounds.*

My clients have identified these healing actions:

- An evening walk with my spouse
- A hot bath
- Listening to relaxing music
- Playing with my children
- Going for a run
- Reading a book I borrowed from the library
- Bringing a brown bag lunch and enjoying time with a friend

Watch out for this phenomenon: more pain equals more susceptibility to fall for bigger toys. Have you noticed that after working extremely hard, you want more expensive vacations, more DVDs, more lattes? And have you heard yourself telling a friend, "Hey, I deserve to have … "

You can't get enough of what you don't really want. Let's face it together. It is not really stuff that we truly want, it's feelings. What do we really want? To feel good—plain and simple. How?

Here are the feelings we want:

- To feel comfortable
- To enjoy new sights and sounds
- To feel proud of ourselves
- To play
- To be heard (this is so valuable that I wrote a book entitled *Be Heard and Be Trusted*)
- To be admired
- To feel loved
- To feel relief from fears and concerns

My own coach suggested that I talk with my sweetheart for us to train each other in how to soothe each other. For example, my sweetheart likes when I massage her feet. That's important for me to know.

And, I like when my sweetheart massages my neck with a plastic massage tool while I'm typing *this sentence*.

Be careful to take care of yourself so you avoid feeling deprived as much as possible. For example, years ago, I only had two suits. But they were good suits. So when I wore them I felt good.

One important way to nurture yourself is to direct your attention to all the blessings already in your life. It helps to write down five details you're grateful for—just before you go to sleep each night.

> *I live in the space of thankfulness ... the more thankful*
> *I became, the more my bounty increased. That's*
> *because what you focus on expands, and when you*
> *focus on the goodness in your life, you create more of*
> *it. Opportunities, relationships, even money flowed*
> *my way when I learned to be grateful no matter what*
> *happened in my life. I keep a gratitude journal ...*
> *listing at least five things that I'm grateful for. My list*

includes small pleasures: the feel of Kentucky bluegrass under my feet (like damp silk); a walk in the woods ... My thank-you list also includes things too important to take for granted: an "okay" mammogram, friends who love me ...
- Oprah Winfrey

Principle

Nurture yourself and unleash the flow of positive energy to you and through you.

Power Questions

How can you nurture yourself on a daily basis? What brings relief and peace? (A hot bath, music, quiet time, calling a dear friend or something else?)

CONCLUSION TO CHAPTER FOUR

In Chapter Four, we have covered the T.U.R.N process to help you improve your situation with creditors:

T – Talk
U – Understand
R – Right-size
N – Nurture

Remember to rehearse with friends or family members before you make a call to a creditor. Creditors want to be paid, and if you take action and start making small payments you are on the road to less stress.

In *Chapter Five, Give It A Rest*, we will cover how to bring more peace and comfort to your life by subtracting and not adding to your to-do list. With more peace, you have more strength to do what is necessary to heal your relationship with the offended person.

Let's flow forward ...

Tom Marcoux

CHAPTER FIVE: GIVE IT A REST

Have you experienced this? You reach for a self-help or business book and something inside feels, "I'm just too tired to read this now."

Some people refer to this as "self-help burnout" or "self-help fatigue."

Why? The reason is often when we reach for a self-help book we're at the end of our rope and depleted of energy. It is just too painful to look at adding something more to your to-do list.

My client Martha told me about feeling overwhelmed. One Sunday, she sat down for the first time that week to enjoy a quiet cup of tea. Then her mother called with a research assignment for Martha to look up multiple Web sites. Her mother wanted Martha to pull together information and give her a cobbled-together report. Martha told me that inside her heart was screaming, "I just don't want any more work!"

Here's the good news. We're not looking for you to add something to your to-do list with this focus: Give It a Rest. Instead, in a number of situations, we're asking that you subtract something that's draining your energy.

We will use the R.E.S.T. process:

R – Relax into it
E – Ease through
S – Sing
T – Thank someone

As I mentioned earlier, the Secret Influence Process includes:
- Strengthen yourself
- Remain in a calm state of being
- Communicate your concern and kindness
- Take action with the F.A.R. methods (forgiveness, amends, regret)

And this section helps you be kind to yourself. When you make sure to renew your energy, you can be at your best and radiate Your Secret Charisma.

Let's step forward gently …

RELAX INTO IT
(#1 of the R.E.S.T. Process)

When I was snorkeling in the Bahamas, I experienced horrible cramps in my legs. I learned something quick: trying to force my way past this pain would not help anything. I had to let go and use my arms to help me move toward the shore. This gave me the lesson that some things cannot be solved with pushing, forcing and extreme effort.

If you see someone resisting your ideas, silently remind yourself to "relax into it." Ask questions and start listening. After you listen to the offended person (for example), he or she may soften a personal stance.

Seeking to relax, many people have experienced the benefits of meditation. I have found that even three minutes of quieting my mind and deep breathing on a train (or plane) transforms my outlook. I feel better!

Some of my clients have noticed that they feel on edge most of the time. A number of them have found the benefit of repeating an affirmation in their mind—and thus developing a positive, healthy mental habit. Here are examples:

- I live in a friendly universe that supports me.
- God holds me safe.
- "Be still and know I am God." (from *The Bible*)
- I feel blessed and peaceful now.

Remember that people who have some daily quiet time become graceful. Graceful people are flexible and can move in any direction. This even brings confidence. You'll start to feel that you can adapt to whatever flows into your life.

Principle
Relax into it.

Power Questions
What are three simple, brief things you can do each day so you experience some relaxation? How can you slow down and relax—and avoid trying to force things?

EASE THROUGH
(#2 of the R.E.S.T. Process)

This part on "Give it a rest" is often about subtracting something. If you want to avoid having your energy drained, pick your battles. Sometimes the best thing is to say nothing.

If it is not a "teaching moment," don't offer advice. A teaching moment is the rare occurrence in which someone actually asks for your help and advice. However, many times when someone asks, "What do you think?" the person is actually looking for agreement.

To avoid resistance, don't start spouting advice without asking permission first. For example, I saw an older man tell a young woman on crutches, "You shouldn't lean on those." The young woman looked up with anger.

Instead, a better approach would include the man saying, "Oh, that looks rough. I remember how a nurse told me a way to avoid some pain with crutches. Would you like to hear her helpful idea?"

If the young woman said, "No, thanks," then the interaction would have remained neutral. If you avoid being judgmental, you can often avoid creating resistance. Then you will not need a breakthrough. Instead, you will have an Ease-through (tm). The Ease-through is a concept I introduced in my book *Nothing Can Stop You This Year*.

The easiest way I can illustrate the Ease-through is by having you imagine a karate move. One opens the hand and slams the palm toward a wooden board. If you take the board out (remove the resistance), you can ease through!

Aikido is the principle of non-resistance. Because it is non-resistant, it is victorious from the beginning. Those with evil intentions or contentious thoughts are instantly vanquished. Aikido is invincible because it contends with nothing ... - Morihei Ueshiba, founder of aikido

When I teach public speaking to graduate students, I show the difference between a karate blocking motion and an aikido motion. The karate block is when force meets force. Then I show an aikido motion in which the attacker is guided to miss the defender and flow past. In this way, I talk about how one can deal with tough questions.

You can turn a question into a gift even though it was thrown like a spear. - Tom Marcoux

The idea, aikido is invincible because it contends with nothing, is helpful as we seek to create healing with an offended person. Hear the person out. Avoid jumping in and defending yourself.

If you are centered, you can move freely. The physical center is your belly; if your mind is set there as well, you are assured of victory in any endeavor ... - Morihei Ueshiba, founder of aikido

What is the real victory? Harmony. Closeness.

Let attackers come any way they like and then blend with them ... - Morihei Ueshiba, founder of aikido

The idea of "blending" with your opponent is a primary method when you interact with the offended person. The offended person, on some level, is expecting you to defend yourself. Don't do it! Listen. After a time, ask, "Is there anything else?"

If you agree in part with what the offended person is saying, the person does not have anything to push against.

To practice aikido properly, you must: Calm the spirit and return to the source. Cleanse the body and spirit by removing all malice, selfishness, and desire ...
- *Morihei Ueshiba, founder of aikido*

Some of my clients express their concern by saying, "But I do have a desire. I want healing between me and my [boss, father, spouse]."

Yes. And the idea is to remove the desire for you to be proven right.

Strong negative emotions can cause you to experience tunnel vision ... Second, strong emotions make you vulnerable to the point that your emotions take control of your behavior ... You risk acting in ways that you will regret.
- *Roger Fisher and Daniel Shapiro*

This is the reason that we need you to take extra good care of yourself. We want you to build up positive "reflexes." When negative emotions rise up or even if your positive desire for healing shakes you up, practice deep breathing.

You can repeat silently to yourself: "Calm ... peace ... center."

The idea is to avoid resisting another person. You can also avoid creating resistance. This is the reason I developed Non-Correcting Conversation™.

The Power of Non-Correcting Conversation

When we love someone, we tend to try to help the person to avoid pain. The problem is that when we talk with them, we sound as if we're correcting the person. We mention what is not ideal ("You're not exercising enough") and then offer our opinion of what the other person needs to do.

In Non-Correcting Conversation, you ask two simple questions:
- What are you happy about? (This is about the present.)
- What are you looking forward to? (This is about the future.)

Some people you'll encounter seem to be allergic to the word happy. In those cases, you can use alternative questions:

- What is working for you?
- What are you feeling pretty good about?

When dealing with the offended person, the above questions may not help. You can use alternative questions, such as:

- Is there something else I can do now that will help the situation?
- As I'm doing _____, is that helping the situation?

The point is to help the person experience some small amount of positive results in the present.

Certainly, with family members, we want to protect them. My point is that let's make sure to have some Non-Correcting Conversations. Don't let it happen that a family member would say something like, "She's always correcting me." Instead, have conversations that inspire a family member to say, "I really appreciate how my [mom, dad, brother, sister] listens to me."

Principle
Remember to ease through; be sure to have Non-Correcting Conversations.

Power Question
With whom can you practice a Non-Correcting Conversation?

SING
(#3 of the R.E.S.T. Process)

You do not need to literally sing. But that works, too. For example, as I type these words I'm listening to soothing music. Instead of singing, I started to whistle. Yes. Fortunately, no one was nearby.

God respects me when I work, but He loves me when I sing. - Rabindranath Tagore

I'm talking about being carried away with music. Sing, sway, whistle, dance. Come alive!

Just a moment ago, I lifted my hand from the computer keyboard and moved it as if I was conducting a symphony orchestra—I'm still listening to music.

This is the day the Lord has made; let us rejoice and be glad in it. - Psalm 118:24

Happy people have more energy and it is each person's responsibility to increase personal energy. With a surplus of energy, you can bring benevolent energy to each interaction. You can be patient and kind to the offended person.

Do not ask yourself what the world needs; ask yourself what makes you come alive. And then go and do that. Because what the world needs is people who have come alive. - Howard Thurman

Principle
Lift your spirits through music: sing, sway, whistle and dance. Come alive!

Power Questions
How can you make time to enjoy music? Can you include music naturally in your day? Perhaps, while doing household chores?

THANK SOMEONE
(#4 of the R.E.S.T. Process)

What is one of the fastest ways to step away from feeling bad? Shift to being thankful. Thank someone. A friend, yourself, or Higher Power.

If the only prayer you say in your whole life is "thank you," that would suffice. - Meister Eckhart

For years, I have been sharing four simple words that have helped my clients and audiences make an important shift to a positive perception. These are the words: *I am grateful for.*

Pull out your personal journal and write down—in 20 seconds—ten details that you're grateful for: people, experiences, your eyesight, and more.

Every day you can choose to create feelings of wonder, excitement, abundance and gratitude. When you get up in the morning, take a moment to say a prayer of gratitude that you're waking to a day filled with possibilities and that you have the health to enjoy it and the freedom to choose your emotions regardless of what happens. - Peggy McColl

Pick three new things each day that you appreciate about your spouse or significant other and tell him or her. - Mike Robbins

At each meal, my sweetheart and I hold hands and say together, "We're grateful." And, during dinner gatherings, our friends (of various spiritual paths) smile as we all hold hands around the table and say, "We're grateful."

Principle
Thank someone and you'll feel positive that you're enjoying benefits in life.

Power Questions
Who can you thank? How would you thank them and for what? What process or ritual can help you shift quickly to feeling gratitude?

CONCLUSION TO CHAPTER FIVE

In Chapter Five, we have covered the R.E.S.T. process:

R – Relax into it
E – Ease through
S – Sing
T – Thank someone

The central idea is to avoid adding tasks to your to-do list. We are looking to subtract actions that may have led to more resistance and the draining of your energy.

Remember to find ways to enjoy an Ease-through. When you are enjoying more moments of life, you are strengthened. From a calm state of being, you'll be able to do what is necessary to restore your relationship with the offended person.

BONUS SECTION #1: YOUR "POWER OF FIVE"

At this point, I trust that you've noticed my strategy to boil methods down to memorable patterns.

Some examples:

Example #1:
To make it easy to remember, I refer to the F.A.R. process:
- Forgiveness—ask for *forgiveness*.
- Amends—seek to make *amends*.
- Regret—express your *regret*.

My distinction is that you need to do these actions repeatedly until the person "gives in" and finally says, "Okay. Okay. I forgive you."

Example #2:
When it comes to debt, the target is to learn how to turn things around. We will use the T.U.R.N. process:

T – Talk
U – Understand
R – Right-size
N – Nurture

Example #3:
In Chapter Five, we have covered the R.E.S.T. process:

R – Relax into it
E – Ease through
S – Sing
T – Thank someone

The central idea is to avoid adding tasks to your to-do list. We are looking to subtract actions that may have led to more resistance and the draining of your energy.

* * *

Above, my examples were 3 to 4 items in length. I've discovered over decades of coaching clients, graduate students and college students that 5 items works well. Subsequently, I refer to such items as the Top Five Methods. And I refer to the process as "Your Power of Five."

In fact, the Top Five Methods form the cornerstone of my training of what I call "Top Five Group."

To introduce you to the foundational concepts, I'll share the transcript of a video that I placed on YouTube.com in which I introduced the Top Five Group:

"Welcome to Top Five Group. This is an elite video training to help you learn the Top Five Methods in the various categories so that *you are at your best*—whether it's convincing someone, or negotiating, or sales, or even leading a group.

The reason that Top Five Methods are valuable relates to how you can access them because you have had conditioning. You have had coaching. And this is better than reading a book.

Now, I have brought to the world 23 books including *Be Heard and Be Trusted* and *Darkest Secrets of Negotiation Masters*.

But Top Five Group, elite video training, is better because what we're going to do is: I work with you, just like this, talking with you directly. I'm going help you stimulate certain neurons—brain cells—that help you get conditioned so that you do things well and without hesitation.

Now, the Top Five concept came to me when I had to defend myself in a couple of physical confrontations. I had conditioning. I had training. And so I wasn't tangled up in 20 methods. I didn't hesitate. I was able to be successful. I was able to endure and to triumph. And that's the idea of Top Five Group: You learn; you are conditioned with this training. We're working together. Plus I'm going to show you film clips in which you'll see me working with my coaching clients.

And so, the recent research shows that when someone (like you watching me now) sees powerful, effective methods, their brain cells are stimulated. These are the same brain cells that are stimulated in the person doing the successful behavior.

What we're talking about here is mirror neurons. I have a degree in psychology, and I keep up with the recent research. The material supports and inspires the conditioning and the training of this elite video training system known as Top Five Group.

A number of my clients and a number of my audience

members have risen into the Top Five of their industry. You have the ability, with my coaching and this training system, to rise up to higher levels of success, happiness and fulfillment.

I'm glad you're here. Welcome aboard. Let's get started."

* * *

Perhaps, it feels strange to see the above transcript of my video presentation. It's natural for this question to arise: "Well, I'm reading this book. How can I get this power of conditioning yourself and stimulating your neurons to work for me?"

Here are ways you can implement a higher level of learning as you use this book as a springboard.

1) Teach another person what you have learned in this book. As you teach another person, your voicing of the methods aloud imprints them on your subconscious mind. That creates more power than merely reading this book.

2) Rehearse the methods. In order to do better in life, you need to create new behavior patterns. Good rehearsal helps you instill such new patterns.

3) Memorize the short patterns like: "F.A.R.—forgiveness, amends, regret" or "T.U.R.N.—Talk, Understand, Right-size, and nurture."

4) Test yourself. Write down part of the pattern (like "F.A.R.") and see if you can draw from memory the rest of the pattern (forgiveness, amends, regret).

As I mentioned, having a coach and having experiential learning is powerful.

In the meantime you can use the above four methods to

move forward.

* * * * * *

Since we have been discussing Top Five Group, here is one of the topics I cover: "Feel Confident." This is relevant for this book on Your Secret Charisma in that you want the offended person to follow your lead. People tend to follow those people who exude Warm Trust Charisma. And that's developed, in part, with the strategies that follow.

Before I write the script for a video segment for Top Five Group, I write an article. Here is the article for "Feel Confident."

Feel Confident

Confident people are attractive. On the other hand, arrogance repels. How can you get the balance right? You learn to LIVE confidently. So we're going to use the Top Five Methods embodied in the L.I.V.E.S. Process:

L - listen
I - involve your body
V - verify and rehearse
E - encourage help
S - seek "how are YOU doing?"

1. Listen

Listening is a foundation for a successful and fulfilling life.

Becoming a skilled listener is a good road to building up your confidence.

Have you noticed that a significant number of people look

really nervous before an event?

The truth is: Many of us are trying to gear up to *impress* people. That's a lot of pressure.

Here's how you can turn that around:

Don't try to impress people.

Make them feel that you're *impressed* with them.

How?

Listen to them.

Here is my straight-to-the-point process for listening:

It's the A.R.E. Process.

[You can remember it with: *A.R.E. you listening?*]

A - attend
R - reflect
E - engage emotion

a. Attend

Give your full attention. Make sure that your heart faces their heart ("Heart faces heart.")

At times, I begin a conversation with, "I'm listening. What would you like me to know about the situation?" The reason for this beginning is sometimes the situation may have some heat to it. When I listen first, the tension drains from the situation.

Think about it: How often do you get fully listened to? When you do, isn't it a what a relief to have your thoughts and feelings heard without interruption or automatic judgment? You can do that for others by giving them your full attention.

Near the end of a conversation, I ask, "Is there anything else you need me to know?" Again, this is about giving that person my full attention.

b. Reflect

Provide what I call "Reflective Replies." Reflect their concerns and emotions. Say things like: "That sounds frustrating" or "That sounds hard to endure."

Why is this valuable?

First, a speaker often does *not* know if you understand the meaning behind his or her words. Reflective Replies assure the speaker that you understand the meaning. Or if you say something a bit off, the speaker can use other words to clarify his or her meaning.

Second, you do NOT tell another person what he or she is feeling. You provide a gentle phrase: "That sounds . . ."

For example, you might say, "That sounds frustrating." But the person says, "Not frustrating, disappointing."

You can ask, "What disappointed you the most about this situation?" That question signals that you are being fully present with the person in the moment.

c. Engage emotions

Help the person feel it is safe to share his or her feelings. Someone may say, "That driver made me mad." Often, I'll reply, "Okay." For me, "okay" is neutral. I do not have to agree. By saying "okay," I'm communicating, "I'm hearing you. It's okay to feel whatever you're feeling."

I have an elderly relative who has horrible habits when it comes to listening. This guy only pauses between things he wants to say. It does NOT feel safe to express a feeling around him. I have actually said, "You cannot logic me out of my feelings. I get to feel the way I feel about this."

Instead, as a good listener, you make a safe place for the other person to express his or her feelings. Once a person feels heard, often the energy about a situation "cools off."

Listening well is a big part of creating success and fulfillment in our lives.

How do you get loyalty and reliable efforts from other people? Listen to them well.

2. Involve your body

Sometimes, it seems like a person may be thinking: "I can't believe what you say because your body is telling a whole different story!"

I've already mentioned "Heart faces heart." It's surprising how many people do not do this simple motion. Subconsciously we pick up the cues. If someone is facing away from us, something feels wrong. Here's what's wrong: The person is showing us with the body out of alignment that he or she wants to leave.

Many of us have learned to put a deceptive look on our face. But our feet do not lie. Trainers at the F.B.I. reportedly teach their students: "Here's the order of assessing if someone is telling the truth. Look at their feet first, then hands, then face."

Improve your posture.

According to research data, people believe those who stand with a posture that conveys confidence and strength.

Here's a fast way to modify your posture. Imagine that there is a string that runs through your vertebra. Now picture that you pull the string up and attach it to the ceiling. Move your body so your backbone is now straight. Be careful to avoid arching your back. Merely line up your vertebra. When you do that, you feel better, and your posture conveys strength and confidence.

3. Verify and rehearse

To really feel confident that you're ready to give a speech or have a difficult conversation, it's best to rehearse.

With my clients and college students (in my public speaking class), I invite them to imagine their grandmother saying:

"Feeling fear? Rehearse, my dear."

When you rehearse, even just 9 minutes a day, you provide yourself with an advantage.

The next level of ways to reduce nervous feelings is to *Verify*. By this I mean, set up simple ways to test that you have the knowledge for easy retrieval from your memory.

For example, if I was preparing a speech about "Feeling Confident," I would remember the idea of "one LIVES in a confident way." Then I would test myself by writing:

L –
I –
V –
E –
S –

Now it's time to Verify that I remember what each letter stands for:

L - listen
I - involve your body
V - verify and rehearse
E - encourage help
S - seek "how are YOU doing?"

If I fail to recall one of the steps, I simply return to my notes and say the missing detail out loud. Then I write it into the open space on the paper. Later, I give myself another test.

Here's another way to Verify. If you're going to give a speech or have a difficult conversation, write down *"10 Questions I Do Not Want to Answer."* These are the tough questions that you dread. Then write down *2 Possible Answers to Each Tough Question.*

After you complete the above preparation steps, you are *really* prepared. I emphasize to my clients: *Courage is easier when you're prepared.*

You'll feel more confident.

4. Encourage help

I have two words for increasing your confidence: "Get coaching."

In a way, you're getting coaching from me through this book.

I continue to have many mentors through attending workshops, reading books, watching videos and listening to audio programs.

I also have an inner circle of advisors, whom I trust and with whom I discuss project details.

Further, I test ideas by placing them on my blog and gauging responses. I put things into the marketplace and see how they do. I make changes in response to how people react to the material.

I also have my own coaches.

I invite you to rehearse in front of people. Get help. You can even rehearse the opening 2 minutes of a speech by calling a friend on your cell phone. Remember the invitation: "Feeling fear? Rehearse, my dear."

5. Seek "how are YOU doing?"

As a nine-year-old boy, playing the piano for 31 seniors at a retirement home, I was terrified. Why? My focus was on

"How am *I* doing? What if I make a mistake?!"

In later years, I learned to *shift my attention* to the audience and focus on "how are YOU doing?" And "How can I really help and serve you?"

At the beginning of each semester when I teach a college level public speaking class, I start with introducing this focus-point:

We don't need you to be perfect; we DO need you to be genuine.

When you are genuinely paying attention to your audience and you truly seek to be helpful, the audience can feel that. And they will be okay with a mispronounced word or a pause while you gather your thoughts.

Feelings of confidence can arise when you know that you will be helping people feel good in your presence. How do you help them feel good? You listen.

For example: Throughout my speeches, I ask questions, respond to questions, and show that I am fully present. It is about "How are YOU doing?"

* * *

Where does real confidence come from?

A significant part comes from using the above Top Five methods.

Rehearse and verify. Experience that *you know* that you know what to do.

And you get a feeling of being stronger and being able to *adapt*.

True confidence is not the total absence of jittery feelings. You have such feelings because something is important to you. Good!

Actors who experience no jittery feelings before a performance report that the actual performance suffers. Why? They simply did not feel the performance was important enough.

But this is NOT for you.

Recall the importance of what you're doing, *and* convert the energy of jittery feelings into more preparation.

Then you'll really start feeling more confident.

* * * * * *

The Power of a *Principle That Rhymes*

One of the techniques of Top Five Group is the use of a *Principle That Rhymes.*

Why?

You want something to pop in your mind quickly.

Earlier, I mentioned how having a few techniques that are well-prepared helps in a physical confrontation.

The martial art technique of a palm strike instantly presents itself in my mind. I do NOT have to sort through 20 methods.

When you memorize a *Principle That Rhymes*, you have instant access.

Further, research data shows that people actually find a principle stated as a rhyme to be more truthful.

Look at the difference in these two statements:
- If you have a doubt, then drop doing the action.
- If in doubt, leave it out.

According to a study, people found the second statement to be more truthful.

And we notice that it's easier to remember rhymes. When working with clients and college students, I emphasize these Principles:
- If in doubt, leave it out.
- Feeling fear? Rehearse, my dear.
- Worst First.

The third statement, *Worst First*, applies to the value of doing your rehearsal first thing in the morning. First, our willpower is stronger in the morning (as shown in data from Stanford University and elsewhere). Second, rehearsing in the morning engages your subconscious mind to work on the project "in the back of your mind." This is also known as "lateral thinking." Your conscious mind can work on something else, while your subconscious mind keeps processing the first item.

In the training I conduct with Top Five Group, I make sure to provide clients with *Principles that Rhyme*.

Why?

They're easier to remember. Also, if a rhyme jumps to mind, then you can go into effective action quickly. [Yes, I noticed that this rhymes, too . . . *a rhyme jumps to mind*.]

Here are three more useful rhymes/principles.

- Keep score and achieve more.
- Trust is a must.
- Take command, focus your brand.

This book is about repairing personal and business relationships. These above three Principles that Rhyme will help you create and maintain good, empowering relationships.

1. Keep score and achieve more.

Several years ago, my father and I were out running for exercise. I had a speech coming up in a few days. During our conversation, I coined the phrase "Keep Score and Achieve More."

I've learned that one powerful tool to get more done is a Progress Log. For example, yesterday, I reached 197 pages for this book. I was excited that I would reach 200 pages today.

The Progress Log keeps up our morale.

People would not go bowling if they couldn't see the pins drop.
– Zig Ziglar

Find a way to measure what you're doing.

It really helps to separate tasks into *Effort-Goals* and *Result-Goals*.

Here's an example:

Effort-Goal: 9 marketing phone calls a day.
Result-Goal: Gain 3 new clients per week.

Simply put, you can't get the Result-Goal without fulfilling the Effort-Goal. However, many other conditions may prevent the Result-Goal from coming to fruition on your schedule. The other person could be feeling ill or in the midst of a divorce. Your product or service may thus fall to the bottom of her priority list. You don't control that.

You *do* control your efforts.
Remember, *Keep Score and Achieve More.*

2. Trust is a must.

Can people trust you? Do they *know* that they can trust you? One method to develop that trust is for you to have the **3 Cs: Clarity, Consistency, and Compassion.**

Clarity

What people know of you comes from your personal brand. I have been training clients, audiences, and graduate students in personal brand techniques for more than 14 years.

A personal brand is the answer to this question: "What are you best known for?"

In other words, a personal brand is a promise:
- Here's what *you can count on me to do.*
- Here's my view of life.

When you develop personal clarity, you do not waffle about.

For example, for many years I have two specific missions that guide me.
- *Tom's Personal Mission:* "I help people experience enthusiasm, love and wisdom to fulfill big dreams."
- *Tom Marcoux Media, LLC Mission:* "We provide energizing, encouraging edutainment for our good and humankind's rise."

Such clarity guides my actions. And people can trust that!

Decision-making is easy if your values are clear.
– Roy O. Disney (business partner and brother of Walt Disney)

Now I invite you to pull out a journal and write down what is most important to you.

Consistency

Can people predict how you will act? For example, do they know you will be on time (or better yet, a little early) for appointments?

Here's a controversial point.

You choose what you want to be consistent about. For example, recently, author Ben Horowitz said, "It's better to be right than consistent." His point was that, in business, sometimes people get stuck staying with a project or idea that clearly is not working in order to "appear consistent."

We might say, "Choose carefully and avoid misguided consistency." However, there is an overall consistency: "You can count on me to make the tough decisions and put the health of the company and team over my own ego."

That is still useful consistency.

Compassion

Here are two principles upon which we can build an empowered approach to compassion:

People don't care how much you know until they know how much you care. – John C. Maxwell

If you want others to be happy, practice compassion. If you want to be happy, practice compassion. – The Dalai Lama

How are you going to show compassion in your daily life?

3. Take command, focus your brand.

Above I shared details about your personal brand. Another way to look at your personal brand is to answer this question: "What five words come immediately to mind when someone mentions your name?"

It is up to you to "take command." How? Be sure that your personal stories, the things you say, foster the personal brand you want to project.

For example, my client Stephen, carefully chooses his words. He follows the leadership principle: Praise in public; correct in private. One word that would come up when his name is mentioned is: "Respectful." This is one way that he engenders loyalty among those people he leads.

Conclusion to Bonus Section #1

We have covered a number of useful details including:
- It's easier to remember and use a pattern like Top Five Methods.
- Principles that Rhyme provide clarity and empower you.
- It's valuable to "take command and focus your brand."

Let's continue with Bonus Section #2.

BONUS SECTION #2: STRENGTHEN YOURSELF

In this section, I share material I first explored at my blog at www.BeHeardandBeTrusted.com. My goal is to help you empower yourself so you have the strength, patience and endurance to lead an offended person to repairing your relationship together.

In essence you need to be stronger and kinder than the offended person who is upset and vulnerable.

We will explore these topics:

1) Unleash Your Hidden Power for More Success and Fulfillment
2) Feel Your Real Power and Joy – Go for Your "Absolute YES!"
3) How You Benefit when You Stand FOR Yourself
4) How to Use Your True Power: Call the Shot
5) Unleash Your Best Confidence

Topic #1
(Bonus Section #2)
Unleash Your Hidden Power for More Success and Fulfillment

Would you like to increase your chances for more success? Have you heard that being optimistic can help? I'll now share something better! One of my college students recently described me as optimistic. I replied, "Thank you." And I added that I describe myself as an **"Opti-Realist."** That is, I hold the view that I can improve situations in my life by devoting effective action. Such action also calls for me to be coachable.

As a realist, I also know that there are certain things outside my control. I work around those details. For example, an Opti-Realist maintains the humility to face personal weakness and build a realistic and useful plan. Here's a simple example. My plan is to eat in a healthy manner each day. *So I eat salad for breakfast.* Why? Because, according to research at Stanford University (and elsewhere), our willpower is strongest in the morning. So I eat well when I have optimal willpower.

Part of being an Opti-Realist is to monitor how your life is going. The fast way to do this is with the question: *Does this strengthen me?*

If the answer is "yes", then keep doing what you're doing. If the answer is "No. This actually weakens me," then *stop* that behavior or event in your life.

Upon facing the realistic elements in your life, then you can form a realistic (and proactive) plan and take effective action. **The optimistic part is that you hold to the faith that**

you can make things better. With such hope, you can accomplish a lot!

Now, we'll use the three methods of the O.W.N. process:

O – open your eyes
W – work around "what is"
N – nurture your actions

1. Open your eyes

Never doubt that a small group of thoughtful, committed citizens can change the world; indeed, it's the only thing that ever has. – Margaret Mead

When I say "open your eyes," I'm suggesting that you open your eyes to new possibilities. Some of these possibilities take form when we team up with others.

I invite you to gain supporters: perhaps, certain friends or a personal coach. If you're going into a new area, you may need instructors and advisors.

The Opti-Realist gets the training he or she needs.

2. Work around "what is"

As an Opti-Realist, I note that there are some things that I do NOT influence.

I do not control other people's moods or whether they have limited thinking. It's intense how I have actually seen friends cut down my efforts and call them "not normal." I reply that my devotion on weekends to getting projects done is "unusual." I realize that I simply want DIFFERENT things than certain criticizers. I'm not interested in being normal. I'm interested in being an Opti-Realist, a leader and someone who gets big, creative projects done.

I **work around** the limited thinking of certain people. Sometimes, it is necessary to reduce my time around negative people, whether they are extended family or some friends.

3. Nurture your actions

A number of people refer to the Law of Attraction—the idea that "like attracts like." A popular book suggests that people need to "Ask, Believe, Receive."

One author suggested that there is a "Law of Creation." In fact, as a college instructor of Comparative Religion for over a decade, I've noted a number of spiritual paths that suggest that *people co-create* their lives with Higher Power.

When I say, "Nurture your actions," I mean that you need to take good care of yourself and how you implement your plans. You need to take action and be creative. Get the right people around you to support you.

And take action.

Perhaps, a useful re-phrasing is: "Ask, Believe, *Take Effective Action!*—Receive."

The power of being an Opti-Realist is that you face reality and take action to have influence. So you avoid "wishy-washy hope"—instead, you have **Specific, Empowered Hope.** You know you can improve your personal situation because you get coaching, you take action, you get support and you persistently monitor your results—and improve your efforts.

Welcome to the joy and fulfillment of being an Opti-Realist.

* * * * * *

Topic #2
(Bonus Section #2)
Feel Your Real Power and Joy – Go for Your "Absolute YES!"

Do you feel too pressed for time? Are you worried that your life is not progressing fast enough? It's time for you to use the Power of Your "Absolute Yes!"

I'm grateful that I receive several leads and requests for my speeches. Also, every year I do some pro bono (free) work to help people who would not be able to use my company's regular services (high-end speeches and coaching).

It's a blessing to be called to help people.

At the same time, I must make hard decisions because, for all of us, time is limited.

How do we make good decisions?

Ask yourself questions like these:
- Would I do this work if I was not paid?
- Am I excited to help these people?
- Am I excited to do this kind of work?
- Is this aligned with what I most want to do in life?
- Is this the best expression of my unique talents?
- Will this help me build something big that I deeply want in my life?
- Will this help me provide some form of legacy that I leave after my time on earth is done?
- Is this an "Absolute Yes!" to me?

Let's talk about "Absolute Yes!"

If you asked me, "Tom, what is your Absolute Yes?" I'd reply: "Jack AngelSword." [That's my reply related to my work.]

Jack AngelSword is my franchise of graphic novels, text novels, and ultimately feature films. The first trilogy takes place in such locations as Mayan Ruins, underwater at Grand Cayman, Japan and Venice, Italy. [See a 1 minute video of my comments at Mayan Ruins, Mexico, and also when I'm helmet diving like my character "Jack AngelSword Tom Marcoux."]

Because *Jack AngelSword* is an Absolute Yes to me, I work on it literally every day. I keep a notepad in my pocket all day and next to my pillow each night. I'm frequently taking notes on creative ideas that arise in my thoughts.

I have 3 teams working on 3 graphic novels–all simultaneously. Plus, I'm completing the first text-novel of *Jack AngelSword*.

On the other hand, I've noticed that creative people who fail to make time for their Absolute Yes slow down, and their productivity declines. Their morale falls into the mud.

When you devote even just 15 minutes a day to your Absolute Yes, your energy expands. A smile graces your face. You become a magnet for opportunities.

Make space and time for your Absolute Yes!

Yes, you may have to refuse some opportunities. [For more about making space and time in your life, see my book *Reduce Clutter, Enlarge Your Life: How to Free Yourself from Physical and Mental Clutter and Make Space for More Success, Love and Fulfillment.*]

Life calls for tough choices.

But when you decide FOR your Absolute Yes—you get so many blessings.

Devoting time to your Absolute Yes is crucial for living a life of joy and fulfillment.

Start today.

* * * * * *

Topic #3
(Bonus Section #2)
How You Benefit when You Stand FOR Yourself

Want to strengthen yourself and keep up your morale? Learn to Stand FOR Yourself. For example, you might notice that if someone cuts you down your physical well-being deteriorates. You can improve your situation when you Stand FOR Yourself.

For example, some time ago, I was feeling physically ill, and I was in significant pain. On the phone, an elderly family member was berating me. As the person negatively criticized me, I pointed out this criticism and I ended the phone call. During the call, I actually felt physically worse and worse.

It was necessary for me to *stand for myself.*

My friend, I invite you to stand FOR yourself. That is, be your own best friend.

The idea of *stand FOR something* became vivid when I heard about how someone had invited Mother Teresa to join a march against war. "If you have a march FOR peace, I'll join in that," Mother Teresa replied.

How do you know that you are standing for yourself?

The answer is: You purposely stay aware of what you're letting into your life. One of my favorite methods to share with clients is: Ask yourself, "Does this strengthen me?"

As I ended the phone call with the negative family member, I said, "I don't have time for people who cut me down."

You see, it's a choice. You decide how long a phone call lasts; you decide where you put your body. Sure, we have family obligations, but you do not have to stay four hours at an extended family gathering.

There is an area where we must stand for ourselves. We need to make space and time for our dreams and for having fulfilling moments throughout each week. This means so much to me that I wrote a book, *Reduce Clutter, Enlarge Your Life: How to Free Yourself from Physical and Mental Clutter and Make Space for More Success, Love and Fulfillment.*

In that book, I share how to make a life-changing difference. Give yourself something that no one else will do for you—space. In fact, a number of people will likely try to talk you out of new behaviors or habits. Some of their energy-draining comments can include: "Oh, you know how you are. If you clear a space, you just fill it up again." And that person thinks they're helping you?

No!

Creating new habits (like one new book and one old book out of the house), takes personal motivation. The solution is to *avoid talking* to the criticizer about your plan to make new things happen in your life.

Remember, stand *for* yourself.

Only you can protect your own personal energy so that you create a happy and fulfilling life.

Realize that miserable people spread misery.

But when you act as your own best friend, your life fills up with more love and positive energy — that's what you will radiate.

Such good energy becomes a true blessing from you to the world.

And then the world responds with more opportunities for you to enjoy success and fulfillment.

* * * * * *

Topic #4
(Bonus Section #2)

How to Use Your True Power: Call the Shot

Would you like to have better results faster? Now, I'll share the strategies of effectively "calling the shot."

Here's a famous instance of "calling the shot": Babe Ruth pointed to the center field bleachers and then hit a home run *to center field*. In essence, he said, "That's what I'm going to do." And he did it.

When working with clients, I invite them to "call the shot" at the beginning of their day. It can be as simple as saying, "I'm going for a 20 minute walk during my lunch hour today." Now the person has a plan to live up to.

Similarly, a good leader provides the vision and direction for his or her team. For example, with my own team members, I "call the shot" by saying something like:

- Today, we'll complete the taxes paperwork.
- This afternoon, we'll complete the back cover of the new book.

Each night before I go to sleep, I "call the shots" in advance of my next day: I take two minutes and write down my *Top Six Targets* for the next day. I identify that I'll use the treadmill for 30 minutes and I'll do my sit-ups, pushups, palm strikes and kicks. In calling my shots, I need to live up to them.

What to Do About "Sometimes You'll Be Wrong when You Call a Shot"

It takes both courage and strategy to effectively "call the shots." Look at past behavior so that you do not press for too much and too fast. Call for you (or team members) to stretch, but not too much. In the beginning, make sure that the targets are truly reachable. It's like weightlifting. One starts with lighter weights and gradually builds up to heavier weights.

Sometimes, you'll be wrong. Admit it. You can say, "Okay. I was ambitious for the team. We didn't reach 20 marketing calls, but look at what we did do. We got in 15 marketing calls. That's real progress, and I'm proud of our team."

A Powerful Question that Can Lead To Your Expanded Success

With my clients, I ask this question: "What truth do you need to face?"

Now, I'll ask you about a possible truth you may decide to face:

Where do you need to call the shots in your own life?

Take some steps forward. Hold a vision. Call the shot and step into your better future.

Topic #5
(Bonus Section #2)
Unleash Your Best Confidence

Do you want to feel more confident? Now, I will talk candidly about confidence and how to improve it.

First, we'll need to analyze notions about confidence.

Let's start with a definition. I once heard a guest on a talk show say, "Confidence is that 'stuff' which converts thought to action."

I've learned much about confidence because I began without it! I began as a terribly shy 9-year-old boy, shaking with terror, as I played the piano for 31 seniors in a retirement home. So I went on a quest to gain confidence because I wanted to do big things: direct 136 people to complete a feature film, act in feature films, teach Stanford University MBA students and more.

I've learned from talking with numerous people that they want three things related to confidence:

- "I want to FEEL confident."
- "I want to DO what a confident person does."
- "I want to GET THE RESULTS that a confident person gets."

These above 3 *Confidence Elements* are NOT the same thing.

I'm going to give three brief, memorable answers to these details:

• *I want to FEEL confident.*

Rehearse. Prove to yourself that you're ready for the meeting, networking event, or other situation.

- *I want to DO what a confident person does.*

Observe what a confident person does. How does he or she walk and talk? Find your own way of doing that. Practice. Get coaching.

- *I want to GET THE RESULTS that a confident person gets.*

Do *a lot* of what can get the results you desire. [For example, Jack Canfield and Mark Victor Hansen submitted their book *Chicken Soup for the Soul* to more than 130 publishers until one publisher said, "Yes. I'll publish your book."]

For more about developing your confidence, here's the W.I.N. Process:

W – walk forward despite fear
I – increase action and rehearsal
N – nurture yourself so that you're willing to fail on occasion

1. Walk forward despite fear

Author Barbara Sher taught me to make the next step small to reduce the fear. From that moment forward, I always look to "reduce the downside." That is, each year my team does a number of projects with modest budgets. If one or two do not yield our preferred income, we will *not* be shut down. So even if we're fearful that a project may not succeed, we can still take appropriate risks. In others word, we walk forward despite fear.

2. Increase action and rehearsal

When you rehearse, you naturally start to feel more confident. Why? Because as you prepare you start to realize that you've increased your readiness to do a good job.

With my clients and college students (in my public speaking classes), I emphasize, "When you're afraid, rehearse."

3. Nurture yourself so that you're willing to fail on occasion

When I first taught college 14 years ago, I made some mistakes. For example, I told certain stories that a business audience would love, but college students found no connection to such stories.

Since that time, I've learned that to truly become skilled and feel confidence related to those skills, I need to take risks.

Every new venture includes a person doing first-time efforts.

You do not know what you do NOT know — until you step into the arena.

People who accomplish much are those who step forward, face appropriate risks, and learn a lot by gaining real-life, real-time experience.

Ultimately, confidence builds as we gain experience and learn that we can adapt to just about anything.

Confidence is NOT about the absence of fear or discomfort.

Real confidence is about knowing that you know (through rehearsal) and also strategizing so that you'll do fine even if outcomes sometimes disappoint.

With enough proactive action and good strategy, you'll continue to make good results happen.

Your confidence will be based on your ever-growing skill set and your deep knowledge that you *are* truly capable.

A FINAL WORD AND THE SPRINGBOARD TO YOUR DREAMS

Thank you for your attention and efforts. As I mentioned earlier, the Secret Influence process includes:

- Strengthen yourself
- Remain in a calm state of being
- Communicate your concern and kindness
- Take action with the F.A.R. methods (forgiveness, amends, regret)

People who say it cannot be done should not interrupt those who are doing it. - George Bernard Shaw

Remember, Secret Influence is to stay in a calm state of being and then transfer your positive energy to the offended person.

To heal a personal or business relationship after you've made a mistake can be an extended process. The point is to continually nurture yourself and to condition yourself so you're at your best when you radiate Your Secret Charisma. As I mentioned earlier, I look upon Your Secret Charisma as Warm Trust Charisma.

Let's review some details about Warm Trust Charisma:

Warm Trust Charisma is the form of charisma that gives you the true and long-term relationships that create personal fulfillment and success. If you're going to go far in business, you need people to trust you.

Since everyone makes mistakes you need Warm Trust Charisma to ride out the bumpy times in business and personal relationships. That's when you can lose that precious trust. Can you repair any business or personal relationship? With this book you've learned how. I also refer to Warm Trust Charisma as Your Secret Charisma, because it's a form of charisma that is quiet. On the other hand, Magnetic Charisma can feel intimidating. You may feel attracted to some movie star but do you trust that person to pay your mortgage or help you get a good job?

Warm Trust Charisma consists of doing what makes people feel both comfortable and cooperative in your presence. The problem with Magnetic Charisma is that its power may fade with the length of time people are together. But Warm Trust Charisma deepens, if you know how to strengthen a relationship.

Here's a brief summary of the distinction between the two forms of Charisma:

Magnetic Charisma attracts.
Warm Trust Charisma gains cooperation for the long term.

* * *

An interviewer recently asked me, "What is the essence of this book?" I replied, "Using methods of this book, you ensure the other person feels so thoroughly heard that they believe you have regrets and you do want to make amends. They trust you to make up for your mistake."

I invite you to return to these pages again and again to reenergize yourself. You will get more value each time you review the steps covered in this book.

Congratulations on your efforts with this book.

To gain more value from this book, be sure to go through it and develop your own To Do List. Take some action. Any action towards improving skills and enlarging your life is helpful. I often say, "Better than zero."

* * *

Please consider gaining special training through my coaching (phone and in-person), workshops, presentations and Top Five Group Elite Video Training.

As you continue to work toward expanding your financial abundance and fulfillment in life, you are likely to come up against some tough situations. To be supportive I've written a number of books . . .

- Darkest Secrets of Charisma
- Darkest Secrets of Persuasion and Seduction Masters: How to Protect Yourself and Turn the Power to Good
- Darkest Secrets of Negotiation Masters
- Darkest Secrets of Making a Pitch to the Film and Television Industry
- Darkest Secrets of Film Directing
- Darkest Secrets of the Film and Television Industry Every Actor Should Know
- Darkest Secrets of Spiritual Seduction Masters

- Success Secrets of Rich, Smart and Powerful People: How You Can Use Leverage for Business Success

See my blog at
www.BeHeardandBeTrusted.com

The best to you,
Tom
Tom Marcoux,
America's Communication Coach
Motion Picture Director, Actor, Producer, Screenwriter
P.S. See **Free Chapters** of Tom Marcoux's 23 books at http://amzn.to/ZiCTRj

Titles include:
Be Heard and Be Trusted
Nothing Can Stop You This Year
Truth No One Will Tell You
10 Seconds to Wealth
Reduce Clutter, Enlarge Your Life
Wake Up Your Spirit to Prosperity   — and more.
(For coaching, reach Tom Marcoux
at tomsupercoach@gmail.com)

EXCERPT FROM
DARKEST SECRETS OF PERSUASION AND SEDUCTION MASTERS: HOW TO PROTECT YOURSELF AND TURN THE POWER TO GOOD

by Tom Marcoux, America's Communication Coach
Copyright Tom Marcoux

... Now, I am in my 40's, with gray in my hair, and for 27 years I have been taking action to protect people.

And now is the time for me to protect you with the Countermeasures I reveal in this book.

Every human being needs to be able to
break the trance that a Manipulator creates.
You need to make good decisions
so you are safe and you keep growing
—and you are not cut down and crippled.

This Darkest Secrets material is so intense that I first released it only with the counterbalance of my most energizing and uplifting books, *Nothing Can Stop You This Year!* and *10 Seconds to Wealth: Master the Moment Using Your Divine Gifts*.

An interviewer asked me: "Who can be the Manipulator?"

A co-worker, a boss, a salesperson, someone you're dating, and someone you think is a friend.

Now is the time—this very minute—for me to write this book to protect you.

I must speak the truth.

These Darkest Secrets of "persuasion masters" are ...

Wait a minute! Let's say it plainly: These are the Darkest Secrets of masters of manipulation. Throughout this book, I will call these people what they are: Manipulators.

Dictionary.com defines "manipulate" as "To influence or manage shrewdly or deviously.... To tamper with or falsify for personal gain."

In this book, we will look on a manipulator as one who deviously influences someone with no concern about that person's well-being, and who causes harm to that person.

Here is the first Darkest Secret:

**Darkest Secret #1:
Manipulators Make You Hurt
and Then Offer the Salve.**

Manipulators would invite you to go out in the sun for hours and then sell you the salve to soothe your burns. The problem is that we don't notice that this is what they're doing.

For example, you're considering the purchase of a house. A Manipulator asks the question, "So, where would you put your TV?" This question is designed to put you into a trance.

Dictionary.com defines "trance" as "a half-conscious state, seemingly between sleeping and waking, in which ability to function voluntarily may be suspended." Let's condense this: in a trance you may not be able to function freely.

Here is the second Secret:

**Darkest Secret #2:
Manipulators Put You into a Trance.**

To protect yourself, you must learn to use Countermeasures to Break the Trance.

All the Countermeasures (actions you can take to break the trance) in this book will make you stronger and more capable of protecting yourself.

Now, we'll view the third Secret:

**Darkest Secret #3:
Manipulators Care Nothing for You and Human Decency:**

They'll lie, cheat, and do whatever they need to do so they win—but their charm masks all this.

Let's return to the example of a Manipulator selling you a house. A Manipulator does not pause for an instant to see if you can truly afford the new house. The Manipulator would neglect to mention that you will not only have your mortgage payment of $900. There will be additional costs: home repairs, property tax, water, electricity, homeowner's insurance, and more. The Manipulator only emphasizes what he or she knows you want to hear: "Look! $900 is better than the $1500 you're paying for rent, which is just going down the toilet. And the $900 is an investment."

Let's go back to **Darkest Secret #1:**
Manipulators make you hurt and then offer the salve.

The Manipulator has you feeling good about the solution (salve) and feeling bad about your current life situation.

How? A Manipulator will make you hurt through questions such as:
- What bothers you about paying $1500 a month for rent? (The Manipulator will use a derisive tone when he says the word rent.)
- What is not smart about paying rent on someone else's house instead of investing in your own house?
- How do you feel about your children walking in the neighborhood where you live now?

Do you see how these questions are designed to make you hurt enough so that you'll buy?

An interviewer asked me, "Tom, aren't these good arguments for purchasing a house?"

"What we're looking at is the *intention* of the influencer," I replied. "Let's look at our definition of a manipulator as one who deviously influences someone with no concern about that person's well-being, and who causes harm to that person. If the person truly cannot afford the house, he or she will be harmed by buying it. If the manipulator conceals the truth, the manipulator is doing harm. That's the important difference."

Some friends of mine are ethical and helpful real estate agents who truthfully reveal the whole situation and help the purchaser achieve her own goals.

In this book, we are talking about another type of person; that is, unethical Manipulators.

* * *

In any given moment, we need to remember the tactics Manipulators use. We will focus on the word D.A.R.K. so you can remember details easily and protect yourself from Manipulators.

D — Dangle something for nothing
A — Alert to scarcity
R — Reveal the Desperate Hot Button
K — Keep on pushing buttons

1. Dangle Something for Nothing

What do conmen and conwomen do to seize your attention? They make you think you're getting a "steal."

I recently saw a documentary in which a conman on a street in England showed a toy that looked like it was dancing. This fake product was actually dancing because of a hidden, invisible thread. The conman was dangling something for nothing. The Entranced Buyer thought he was getting something worth $20 for only $5. That was the trick. The Entranced Buyer felt that he was getting $15 extra of value for his $5. What the Buyer really got was something worth nothing. Similarly, I know someone who purchased a copy of a Disney movie from a street vendor in San Francisco. She brought the copy home and it was unwatchable—and the street vendor was never seen again.

An old phrase goes, "A conman cannot con someone who is not looking for something for nothing."

How to Protect Yourself from "Dangle Something for Nothing"

Stop! Get on your cell phone and talk through the "deal" with someone you know who thinks clearly. Go home. Think about it. Do some research on the Internet. Listen to your gut feelings. If the salesman or conman is too insistent, get away from that Manipulator. Get quiet. Have a cup of water. Cool down. Break the Trance!

Break the Trance and Identify the Crucial Detail

Earlier, I mentioned that a Manipulator puts you into a trance. An added problem is that we put ourselves into a trance. For example, as you read this, are you thinking about your right toe? Most likely not (unless you stubbed your toe recently). The point is that we only focus on a tiny percentage of what is going on in our life.

Around fifteen years ago, I caused myself trouble because I put myself into a trance. I discovered that under certain conditions, friendship can make you nearly deaf. Here's how: I was producing a song for a motion picture. A good friend was singing backup in the chorus. Because of our friendship, I wanted him to sound great. I completely missed the Crucial Detail. In this kind of situation, the Crucial Detail is that what truly counts is how the lead singer sounds! I made a song that I could not release. What a waste of time and money! I had put myself into a trance.

In any situation in which the Manipulator is "dangling something for nothing," we often fall into a trance and miss the Crucial Detail. The most important detail is *not* that we're saving money if we order before midnight tonight. What counts is whether the product creates a lasting, crucial benefit in our lives. And is the benefit of the product worth the cost? Some people even program themselves to make mistakes by saying, "I can't pass up a bargain." The bargain is *not* the Crucial Detail.

Secrets to Break the Trance

This is the process of B.R.E.A.K.S. It will help you remember the proven methods to break a trance.

B — Breathe
R — Relax
E — Envision
A — Act on aromas
K — Keep moving
S — Smile

Secret #1: Breathe

Remember Secret #1: Manipulators make you hurt and then offer the salve. The Manipulator wants to put you into a state of being that fills you with a sense of urgency and anxiety. Oh, no! I'm going to miss the sale!

Stop this highly vulnerable state. Take a deep breath. Do it now. Take a deep breath and let your belly "get fat" by filling it with air. As you breathe out, let your belly deflate. Breathe in through your nose and breathe out through your